Horses Lovers

Coloring Book for Adults

A Gray Scale Coloring Book

Second Edition

By

Engy Khalil

Copyrighted Material

All Rights Reserved. No part of publication may be reproduced in any form or any means, including photocopying, scanning or another way without prior written permission of the copyright material holder.

Copyrighted © 2017 Engy Khalil

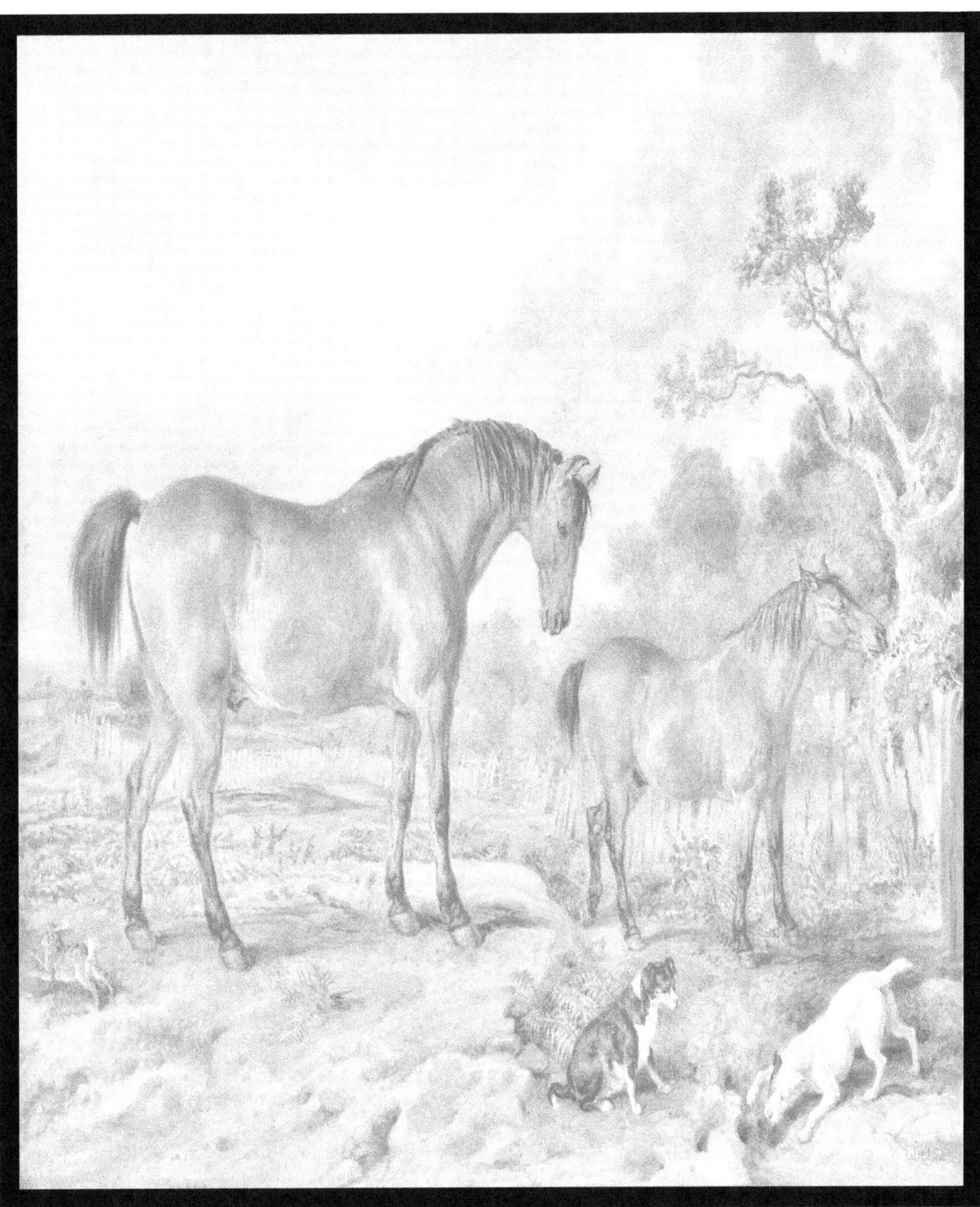

Coloring Book for Adults

Horses Lovers

By

Engy Khalil

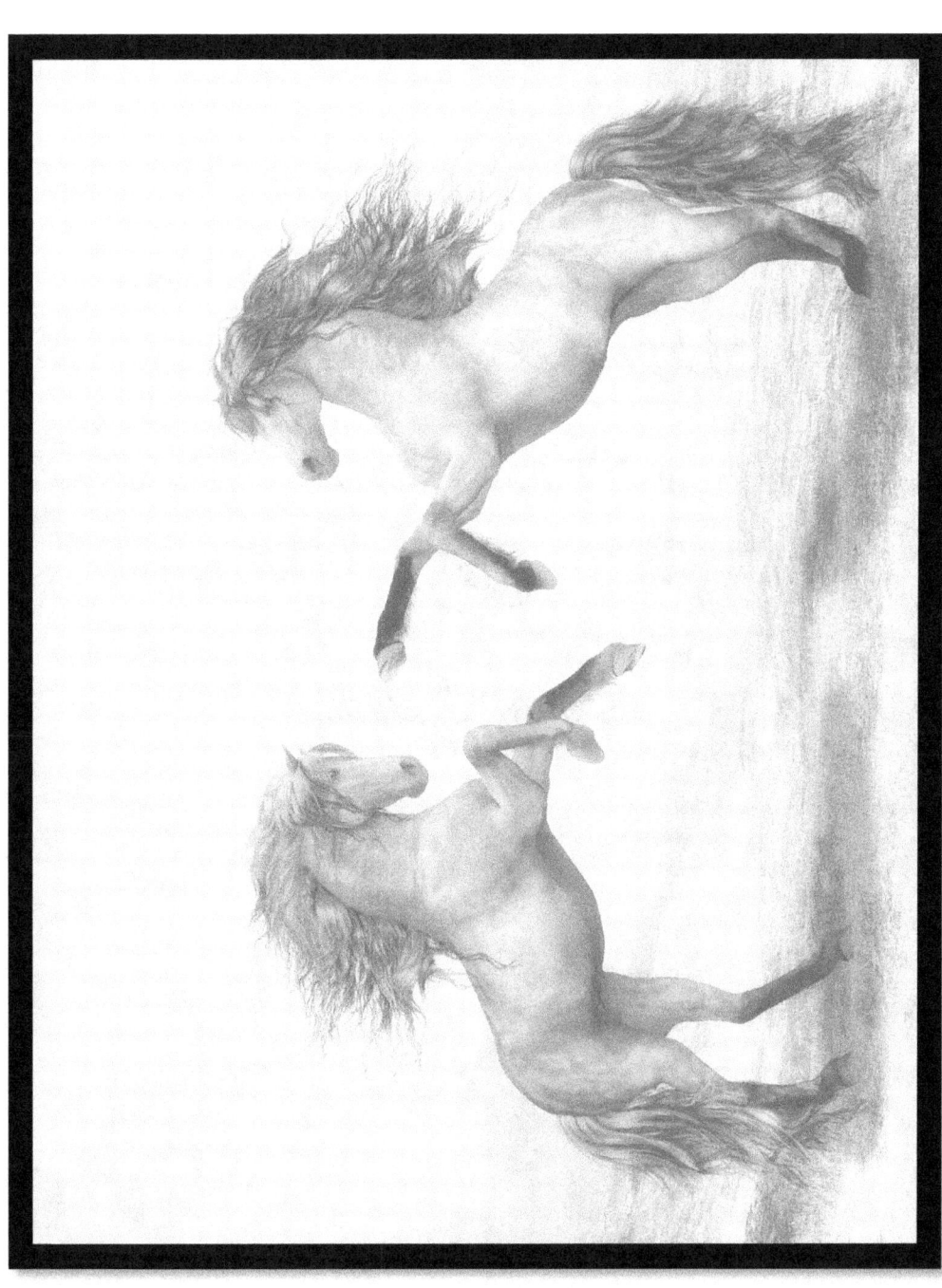

Coloring Book for Adults

Horses Lovers

By

Engy Khalil

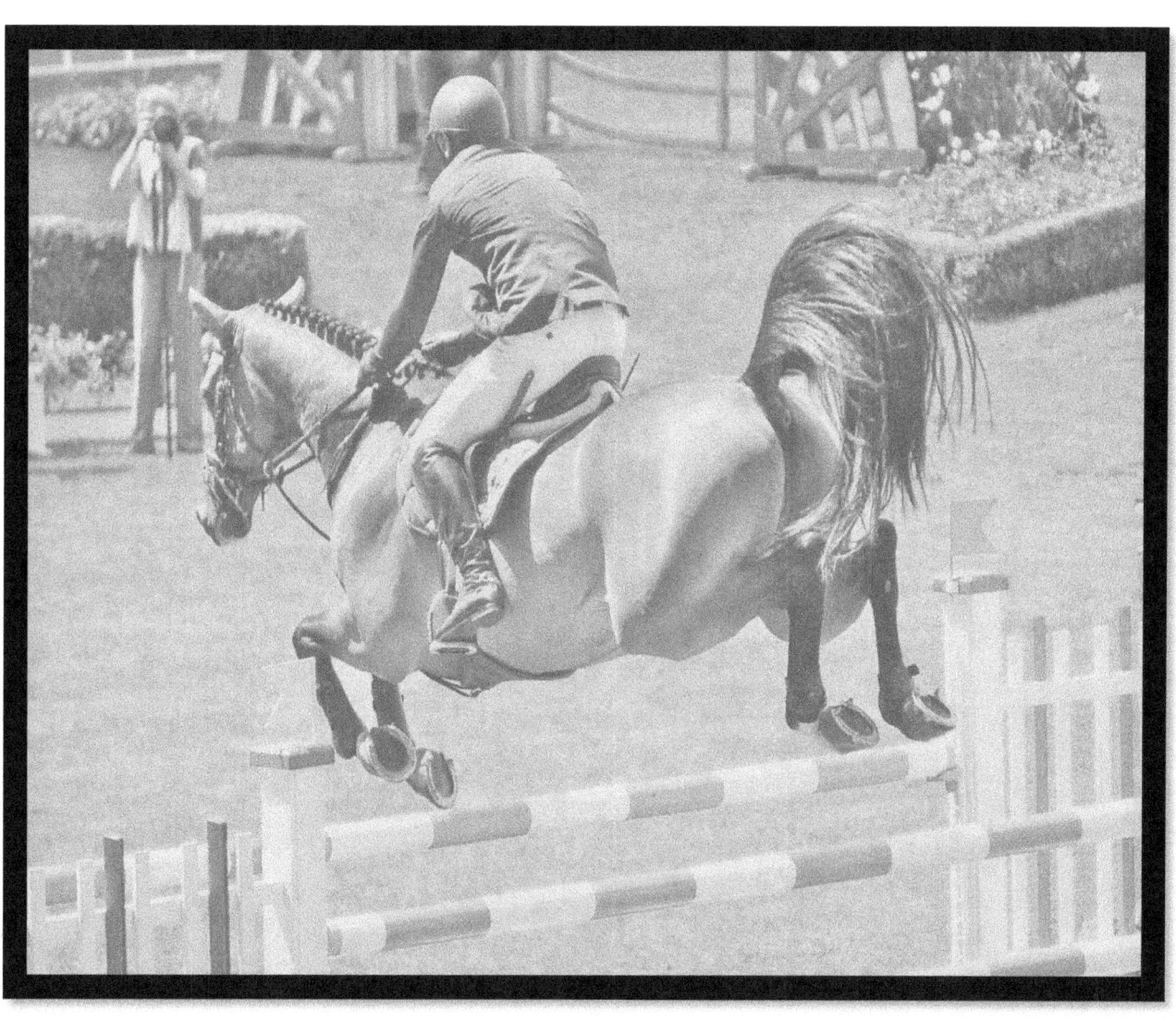

Coloring Book for Adults

Horses Lovers

By

Engy Khalil

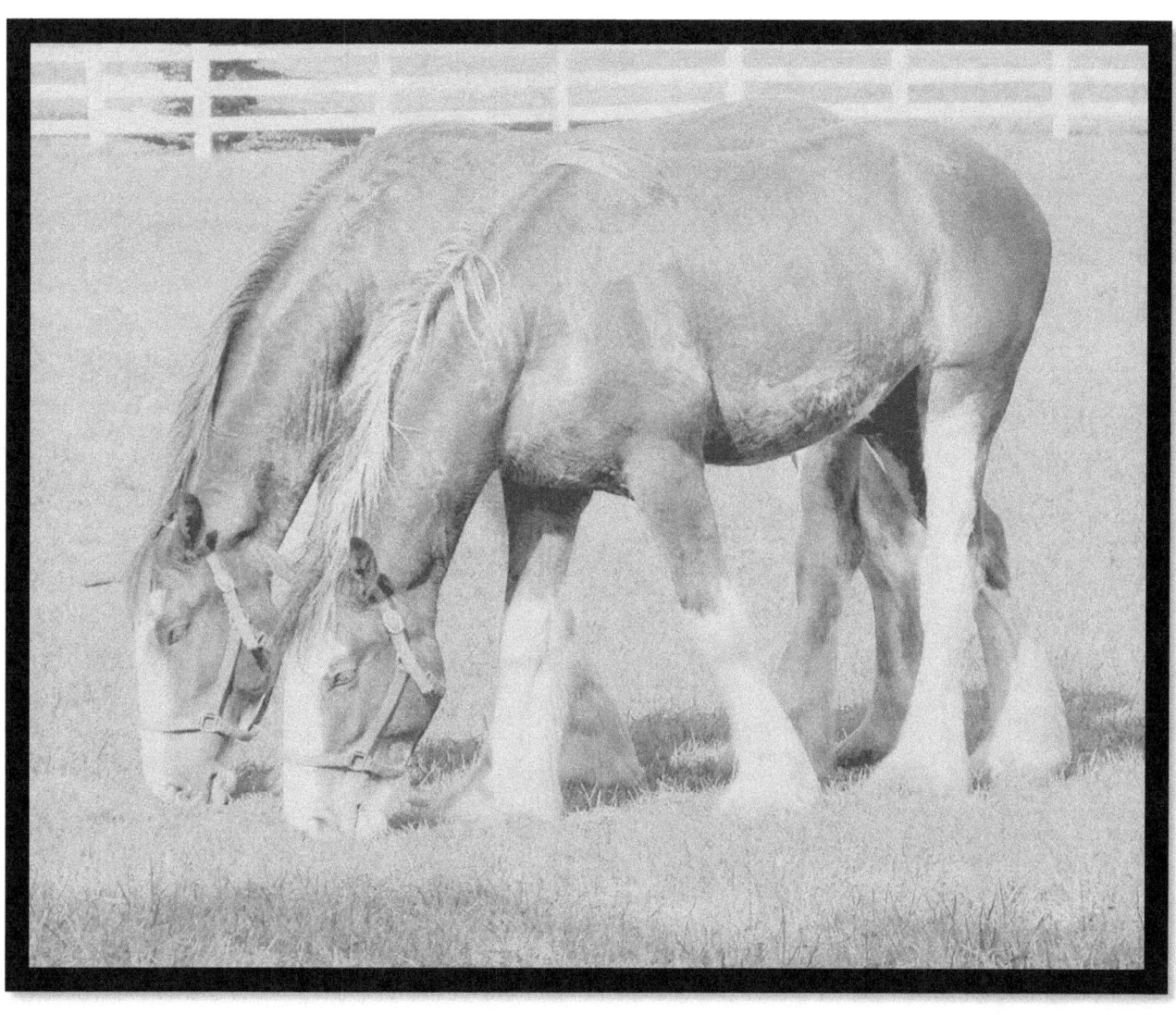

Coloring Book for Adults

Horses Lovers

By

Engy Khalil

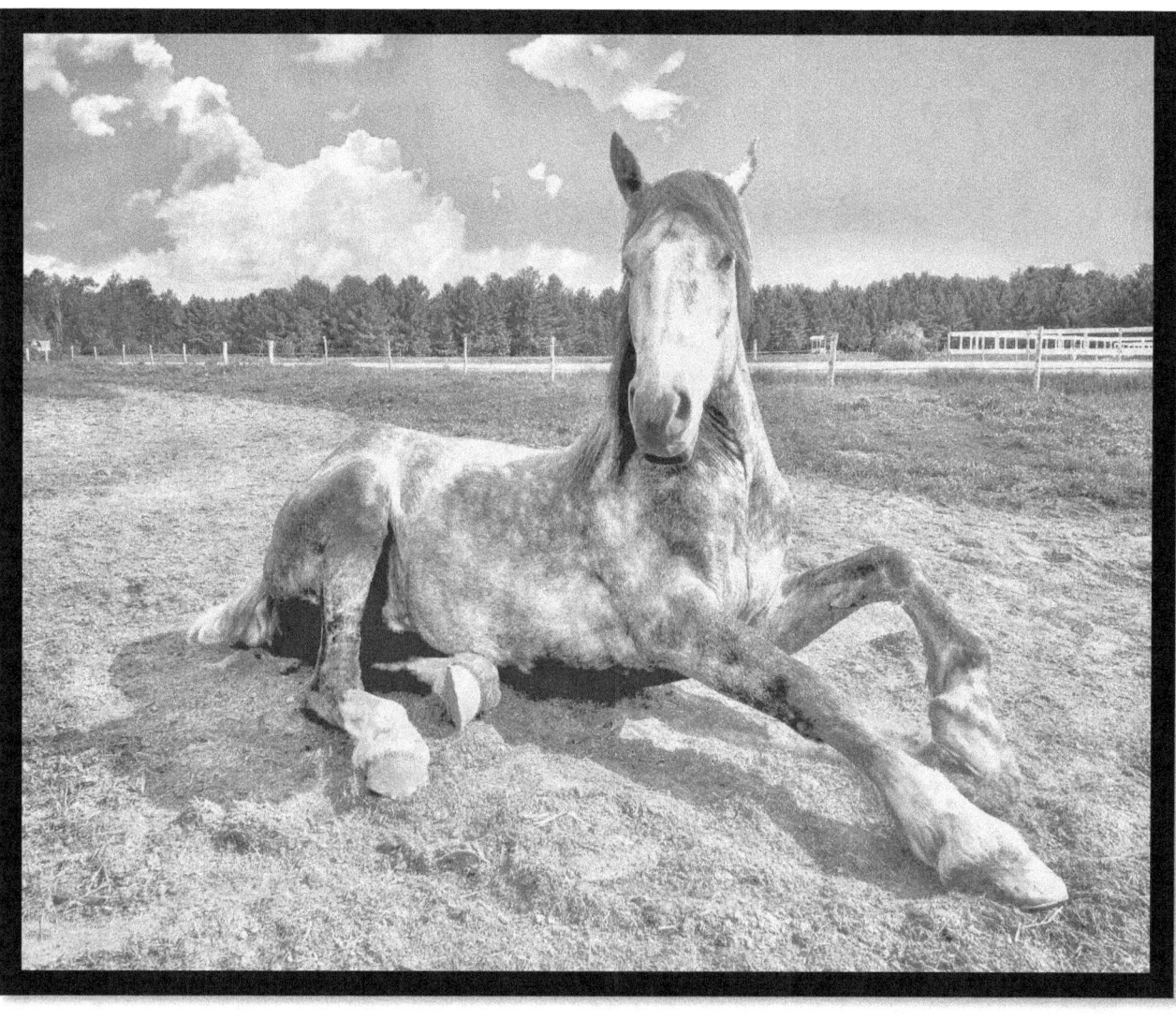

Coloring Book for Adults

Horses Lovers

By

Engy Khalil

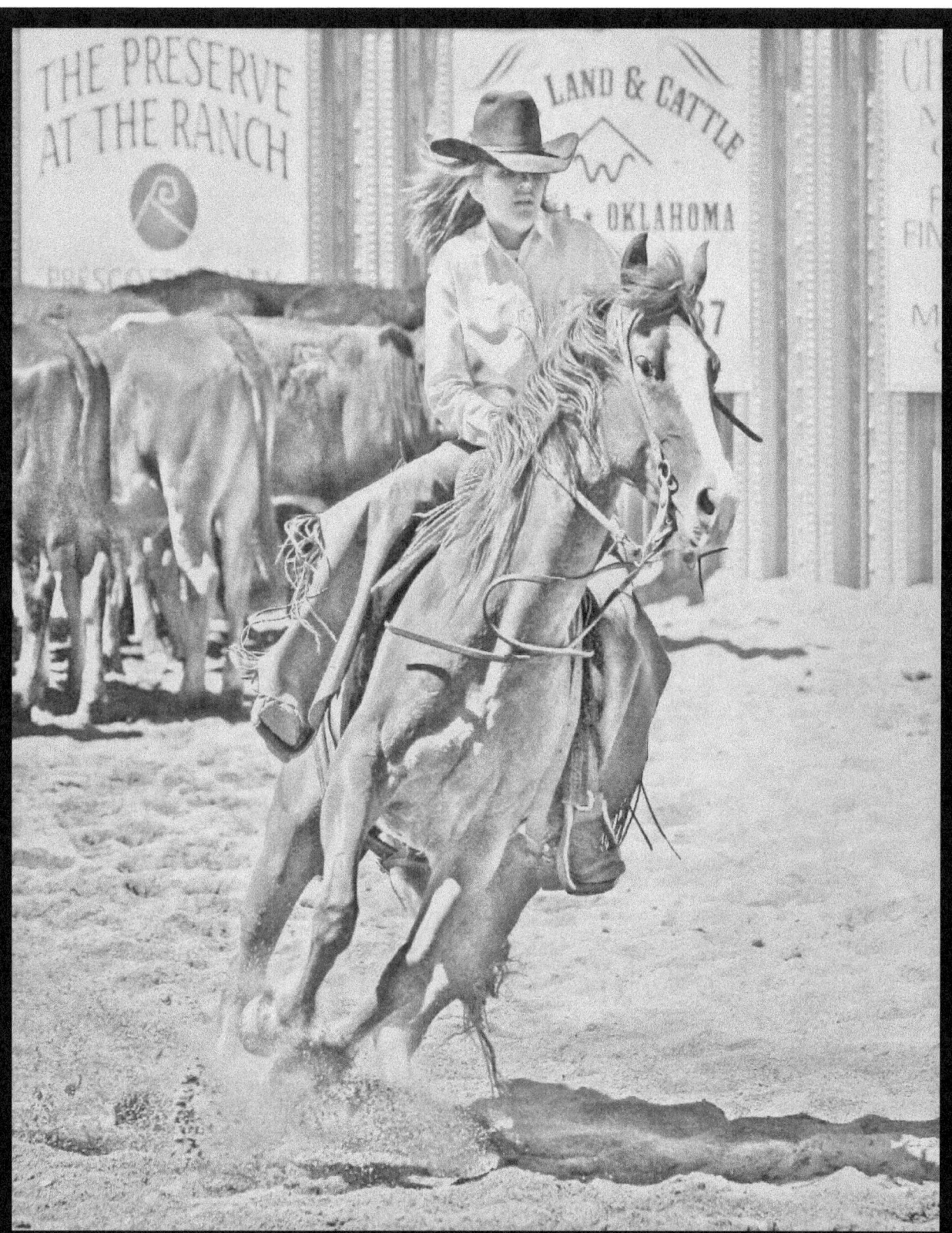

Coloring Book for Adults

Horses Lovers

By

Engy Khalil

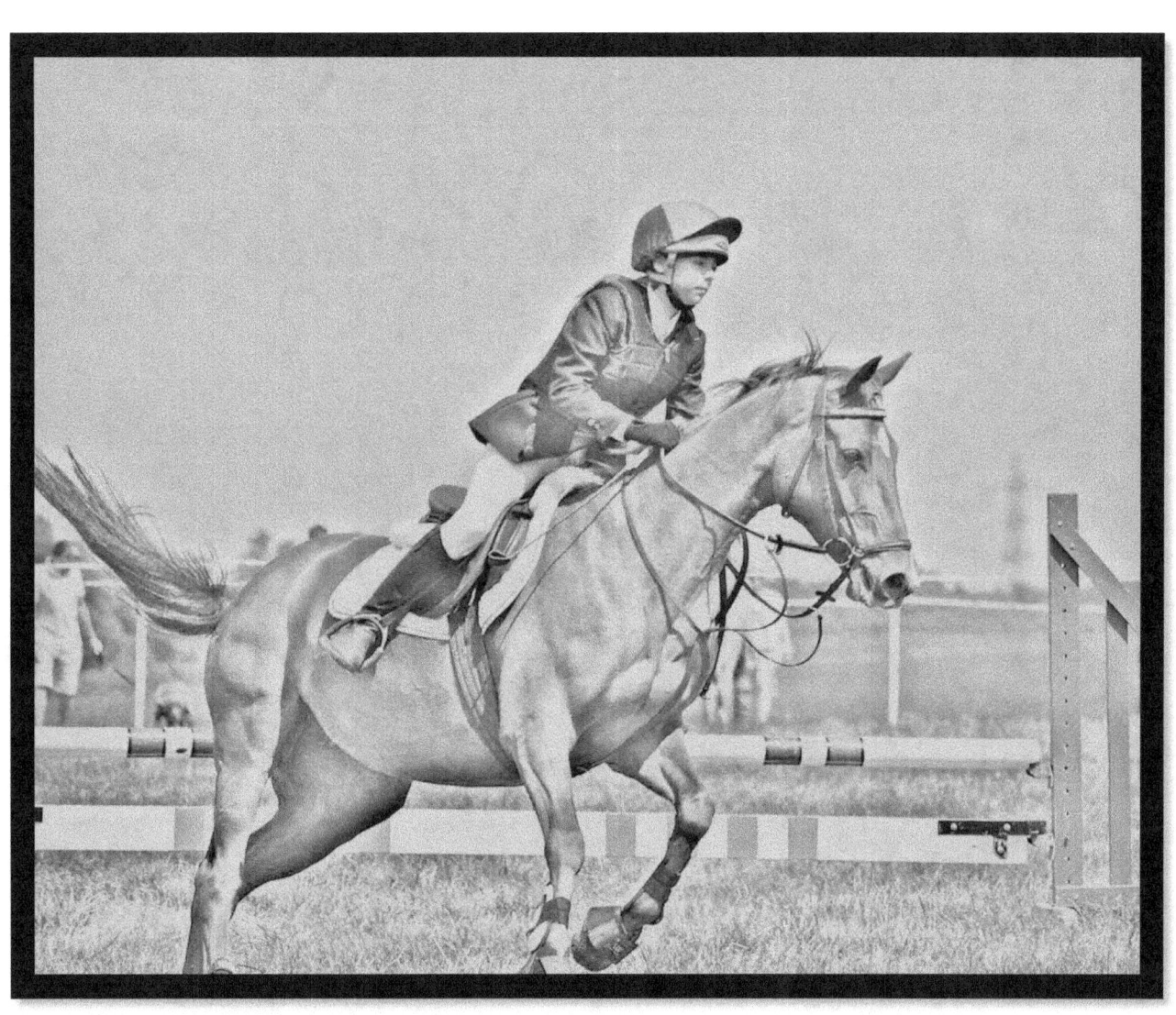

Coloring Book for Adults

Horses Lovers

By

Engy Khalil

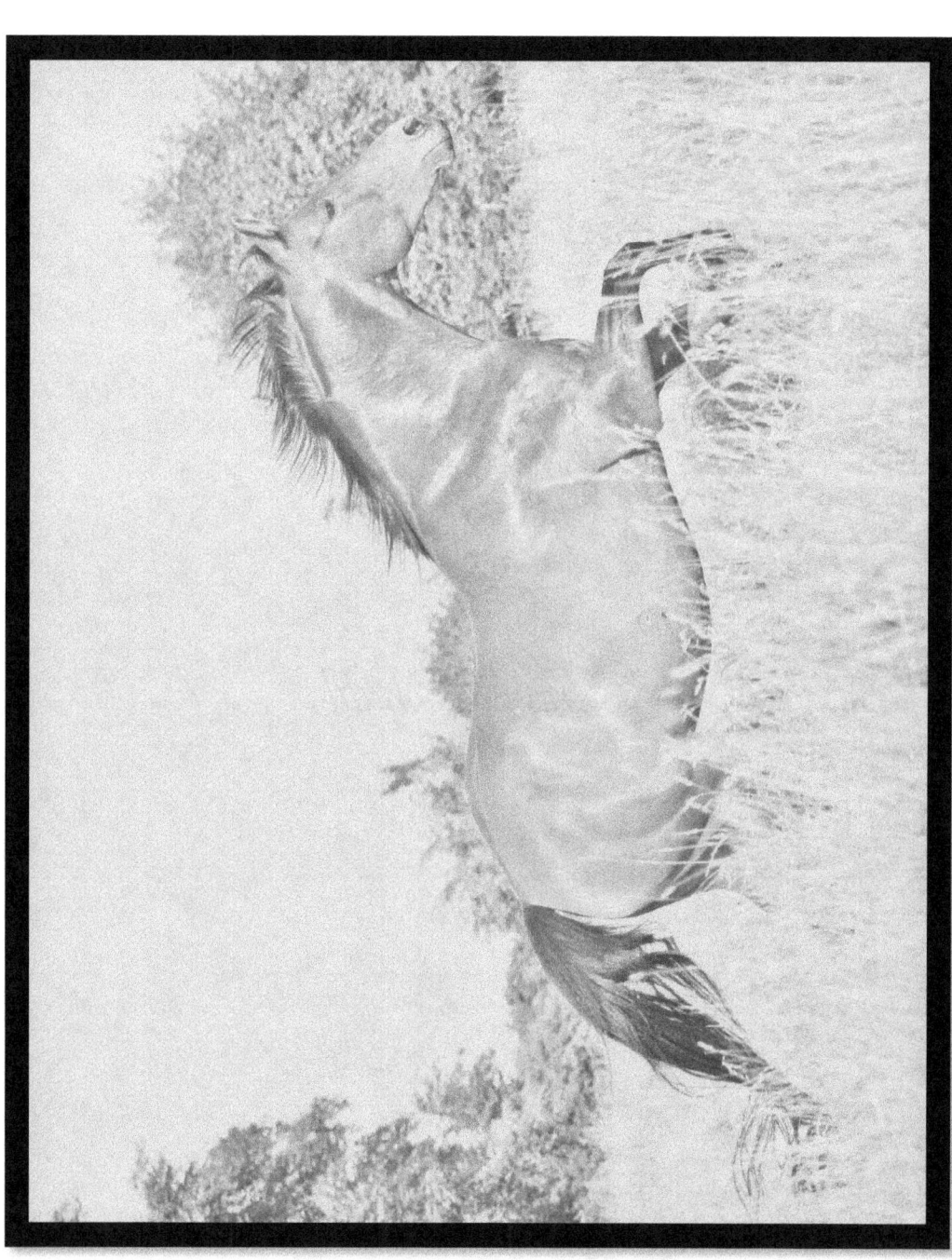

Coloring Book for Adults

Horses Lovers

By

Engy Khalil

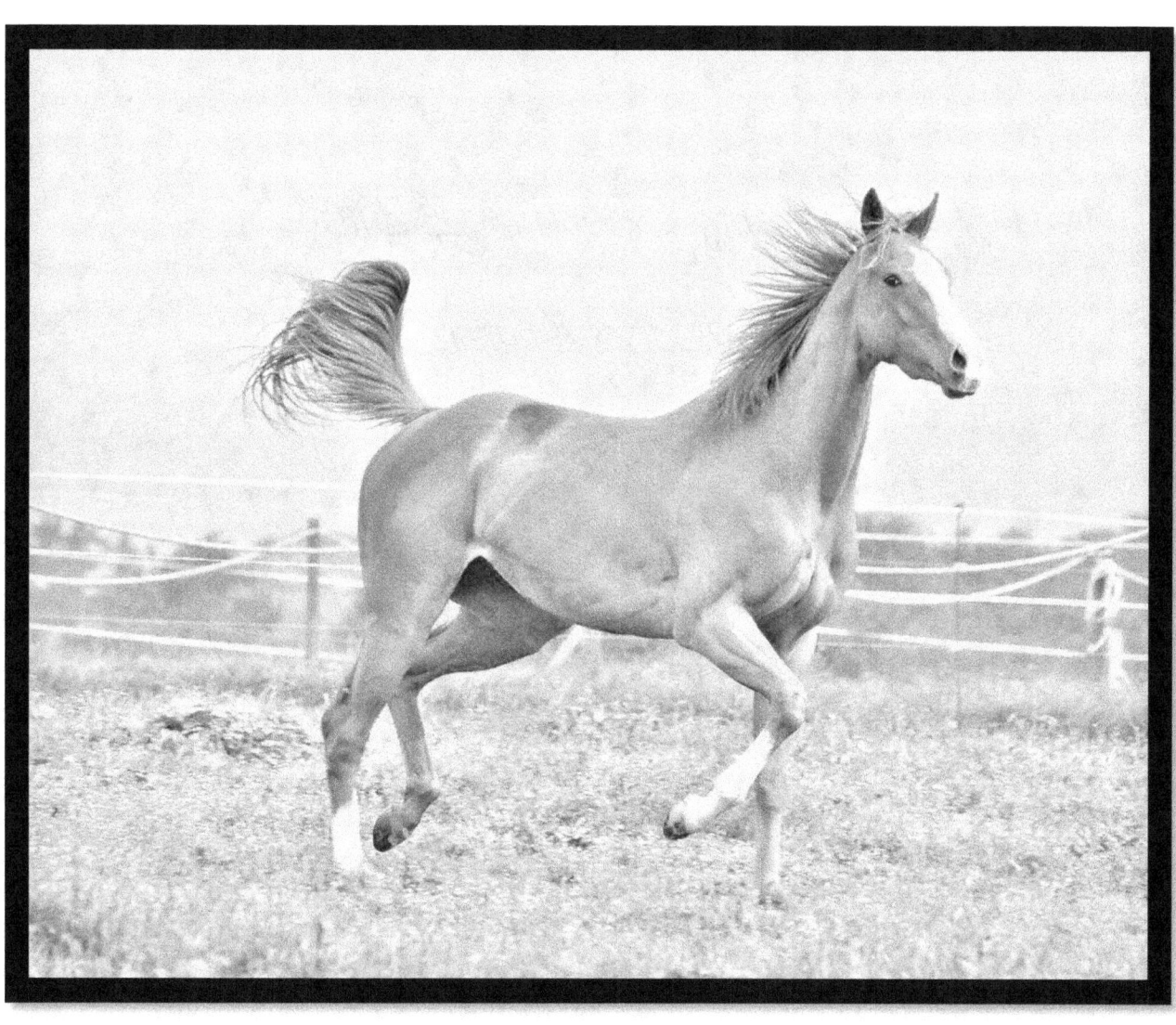

Coloring Book for Adults

Horses Lovers

By

Engy Khalil

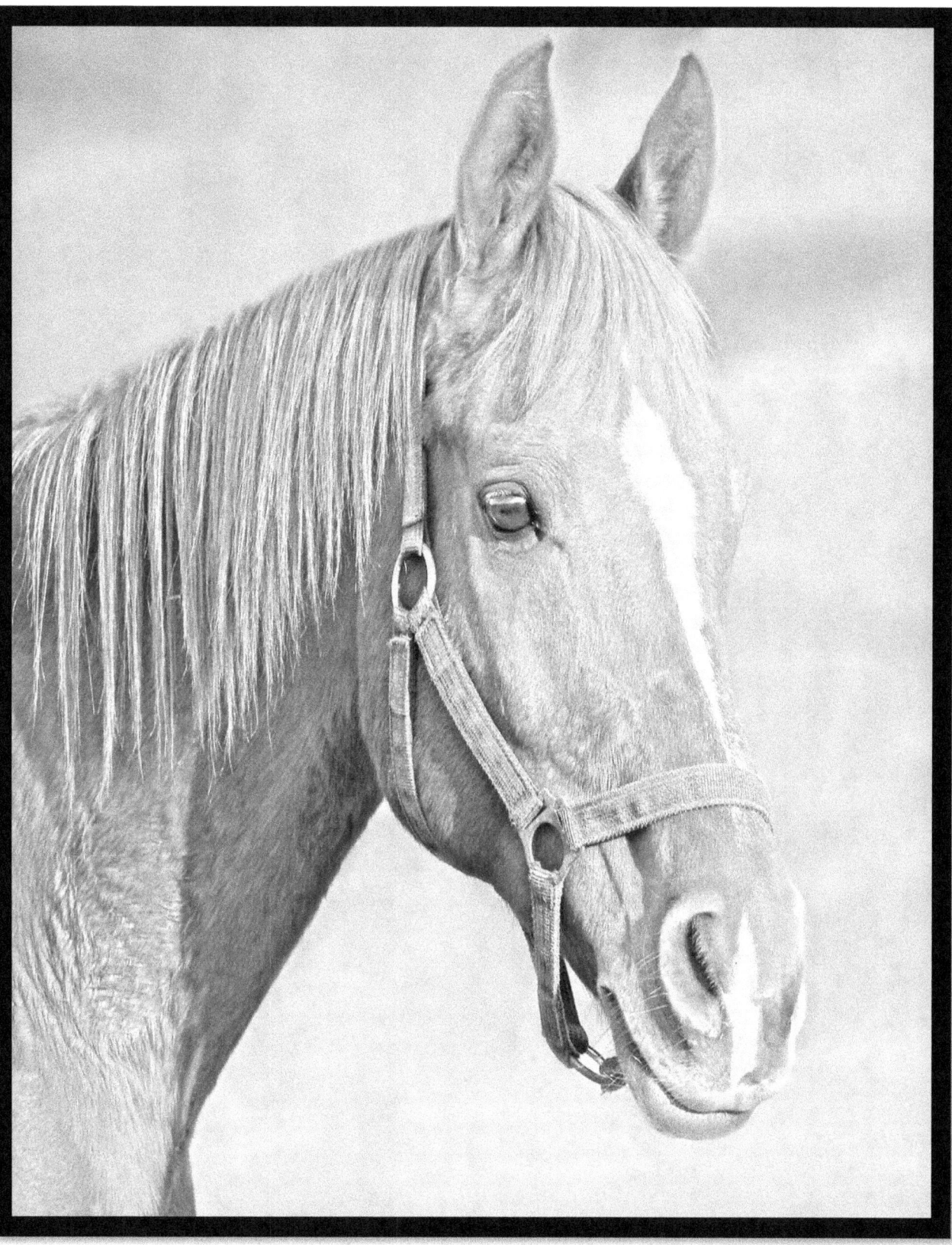

Coloring Book for Adults

Horses Lovers

By

Engy Khalil

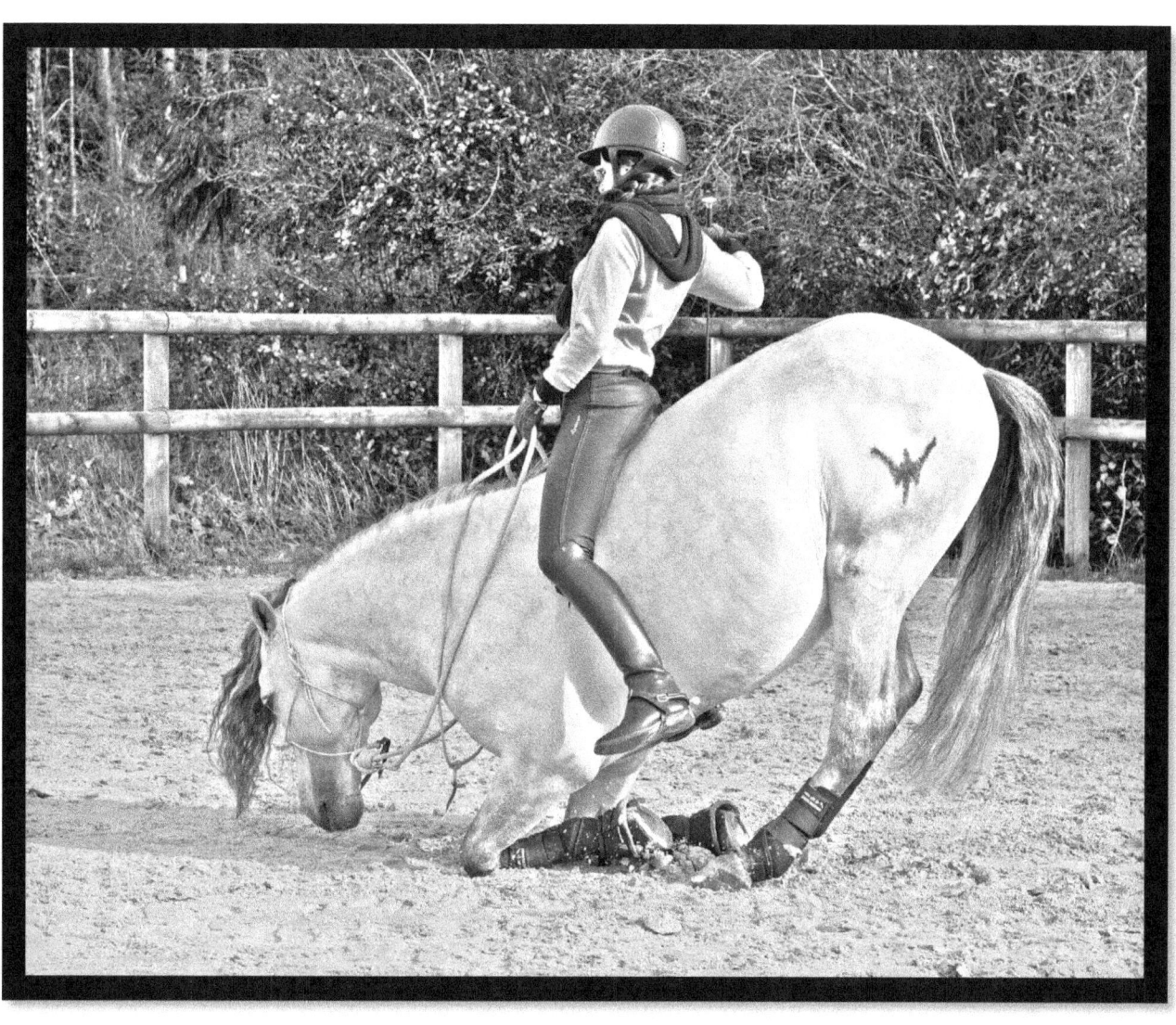

Coloring Book for Adults

Horses Lovers

By

Engy Khalil

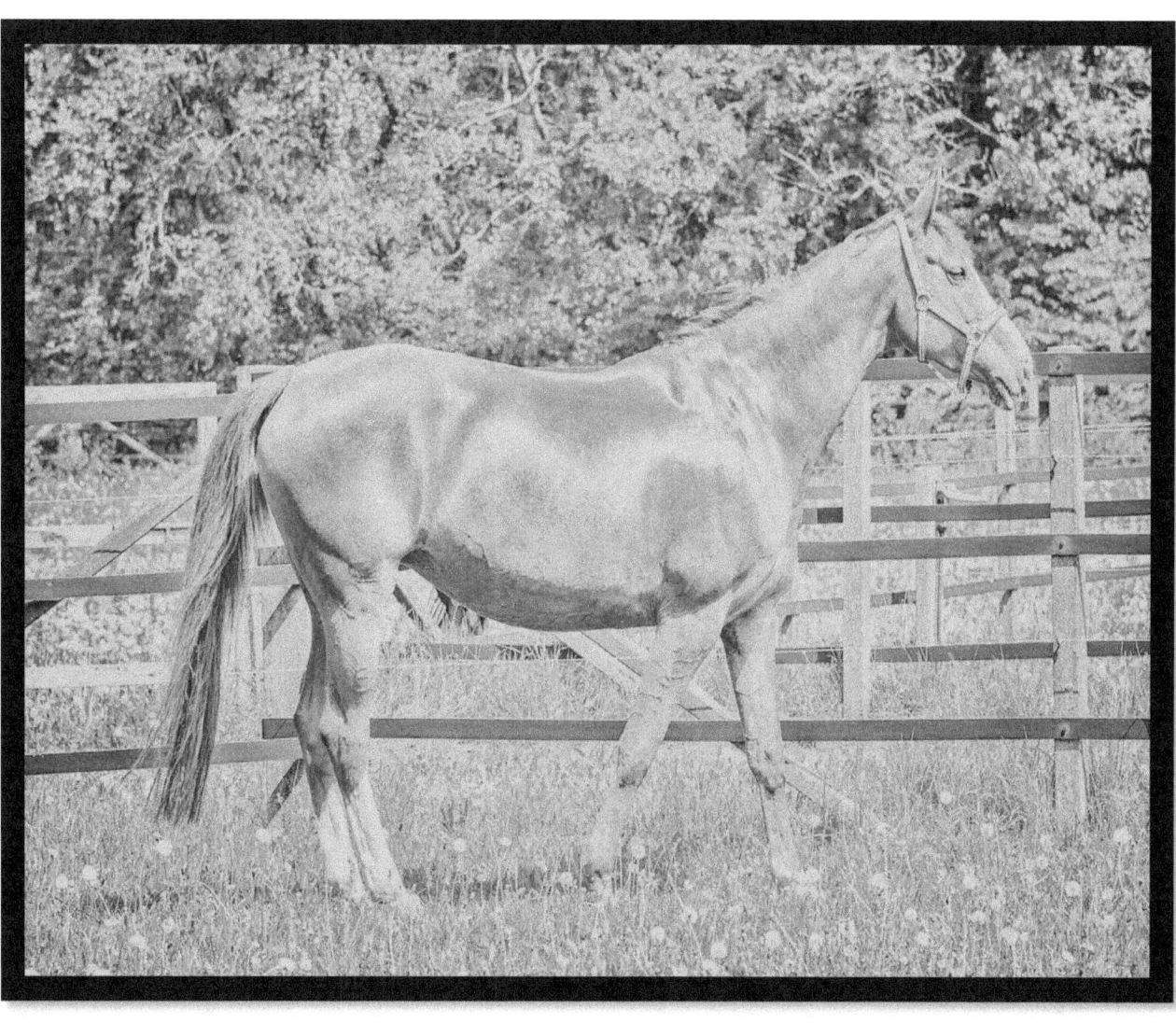

Coloring Book for Adults

Horses Lovers

By

Engy Khalil

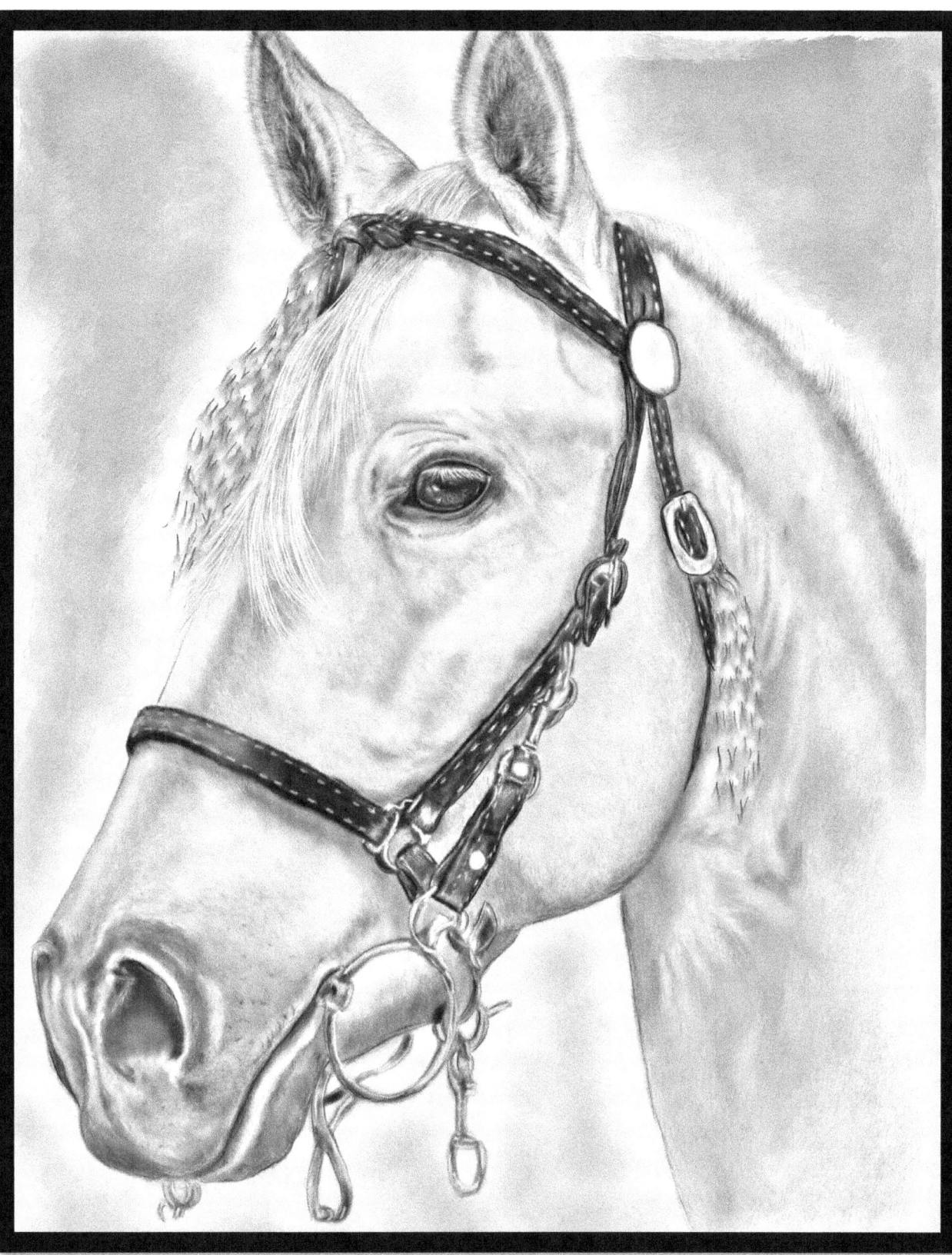

Coloring Book for Adults

Horses Lovers

By

Engy Khalil

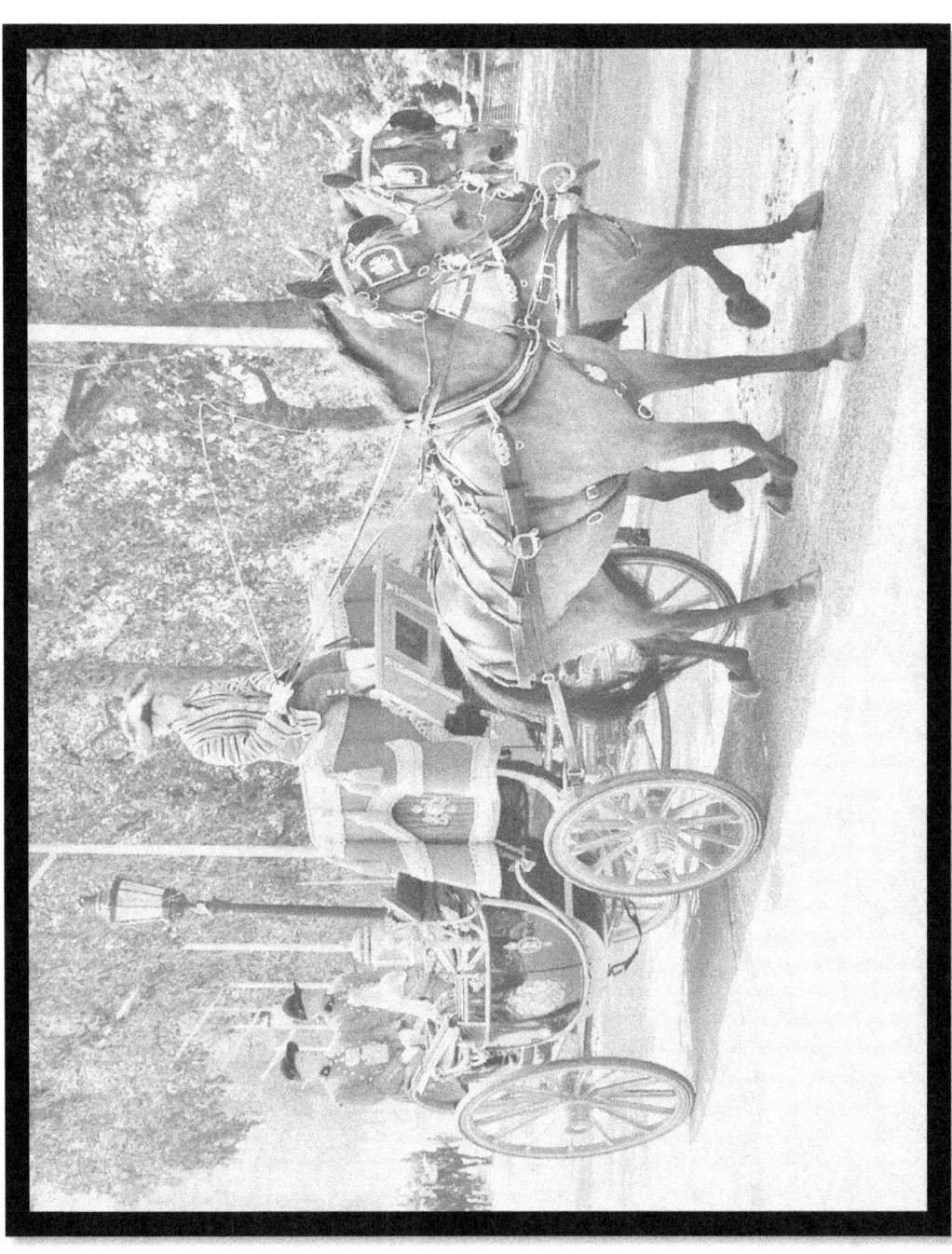

Coloring Book for Adults

Horses Lovers

By

Engy Khalil

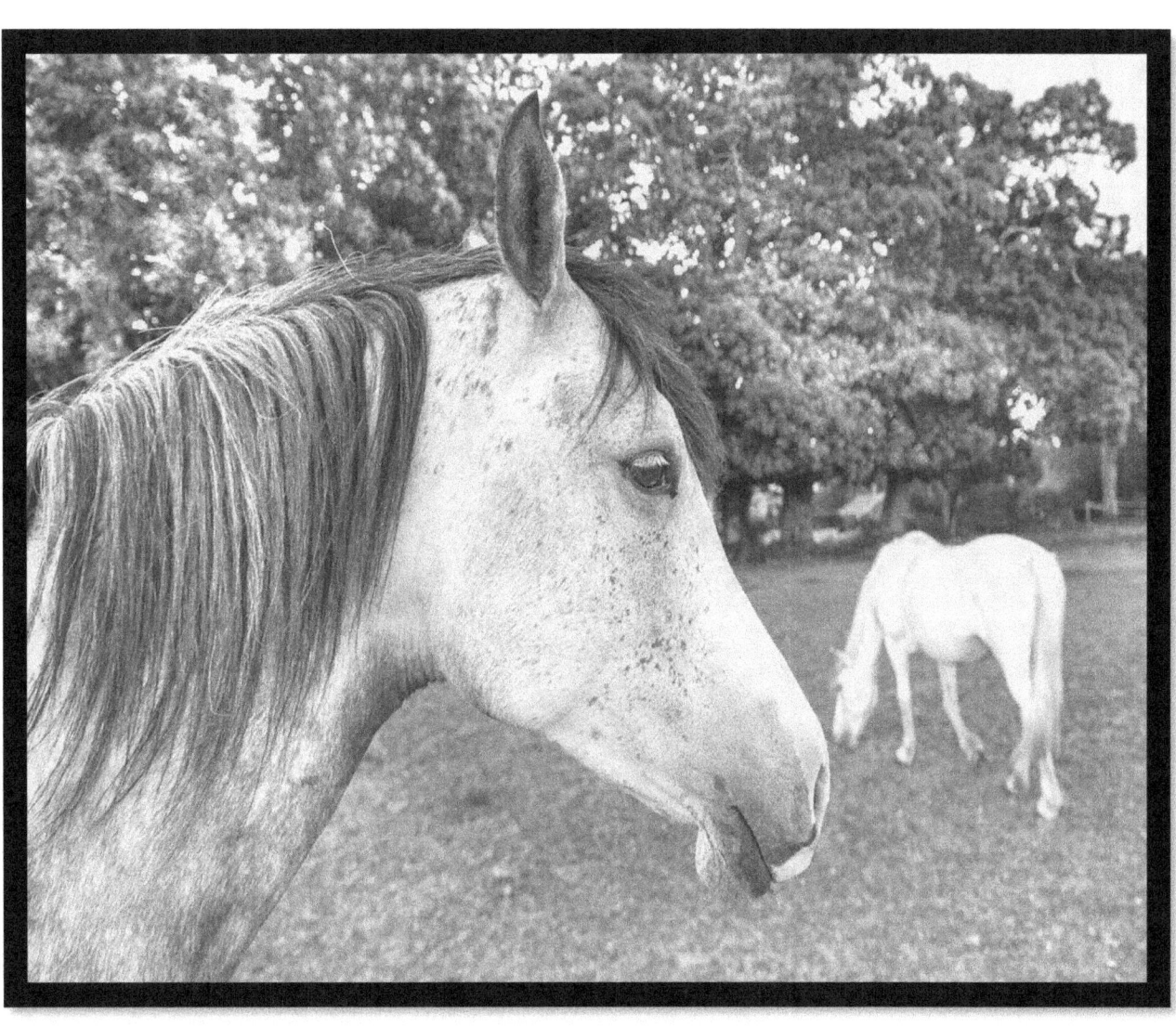

Coloring Book for Adults

Horses Lovers

By

Engy Khalil

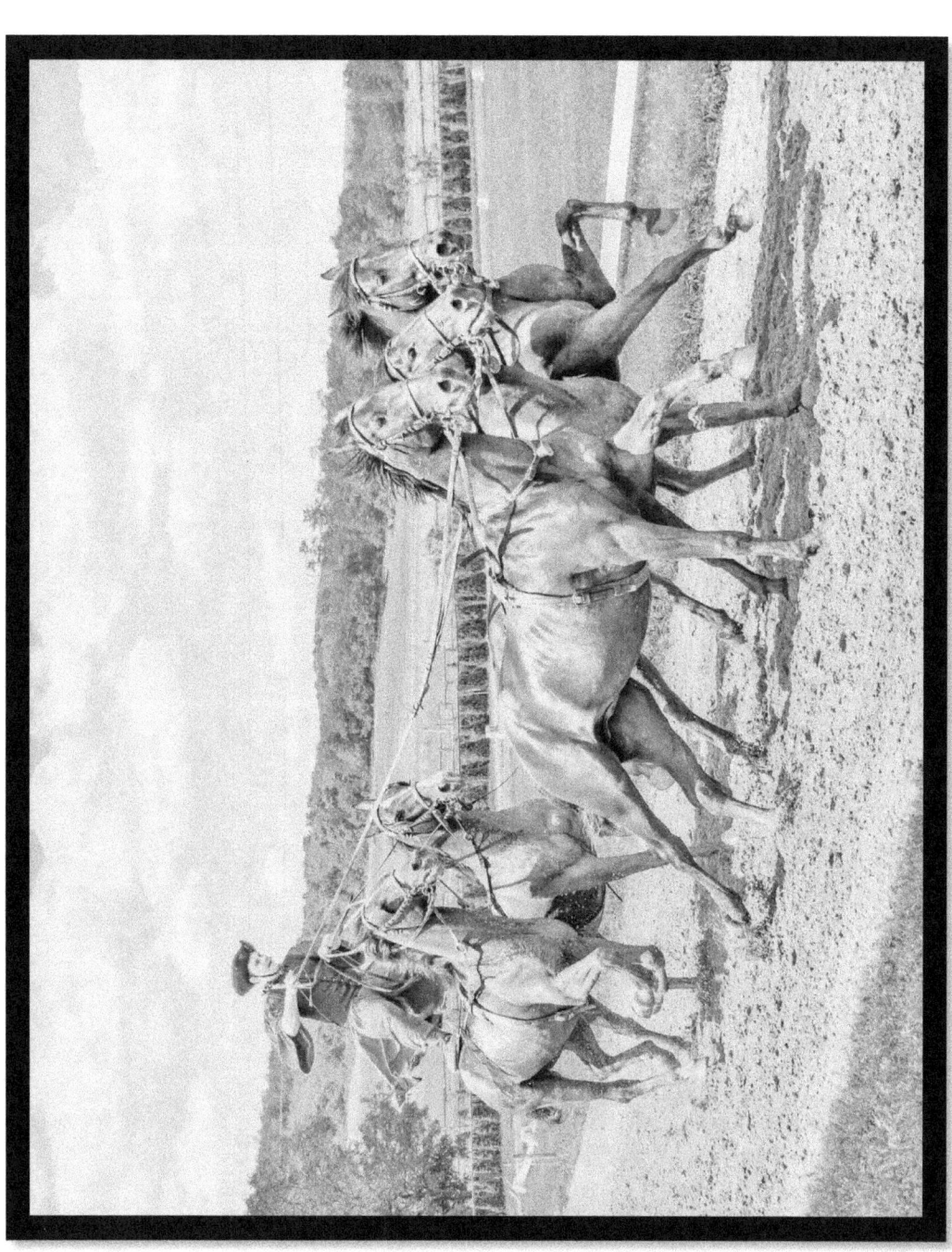

Coloring Book for Adults

Horses Lovers

By

Engy Khalil

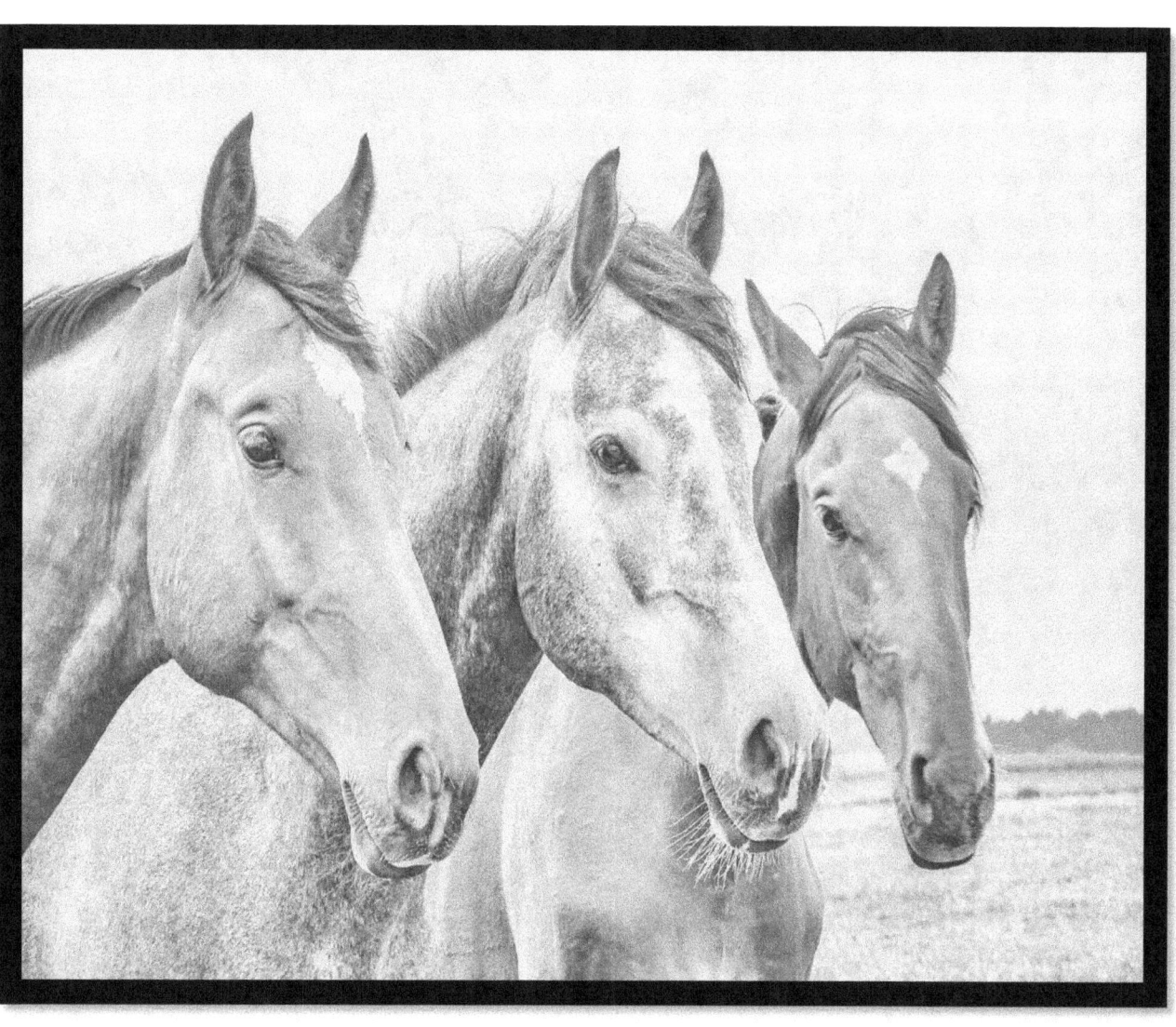

Coloring Book for Adults

Horses Lovers

By

Engy Khalil

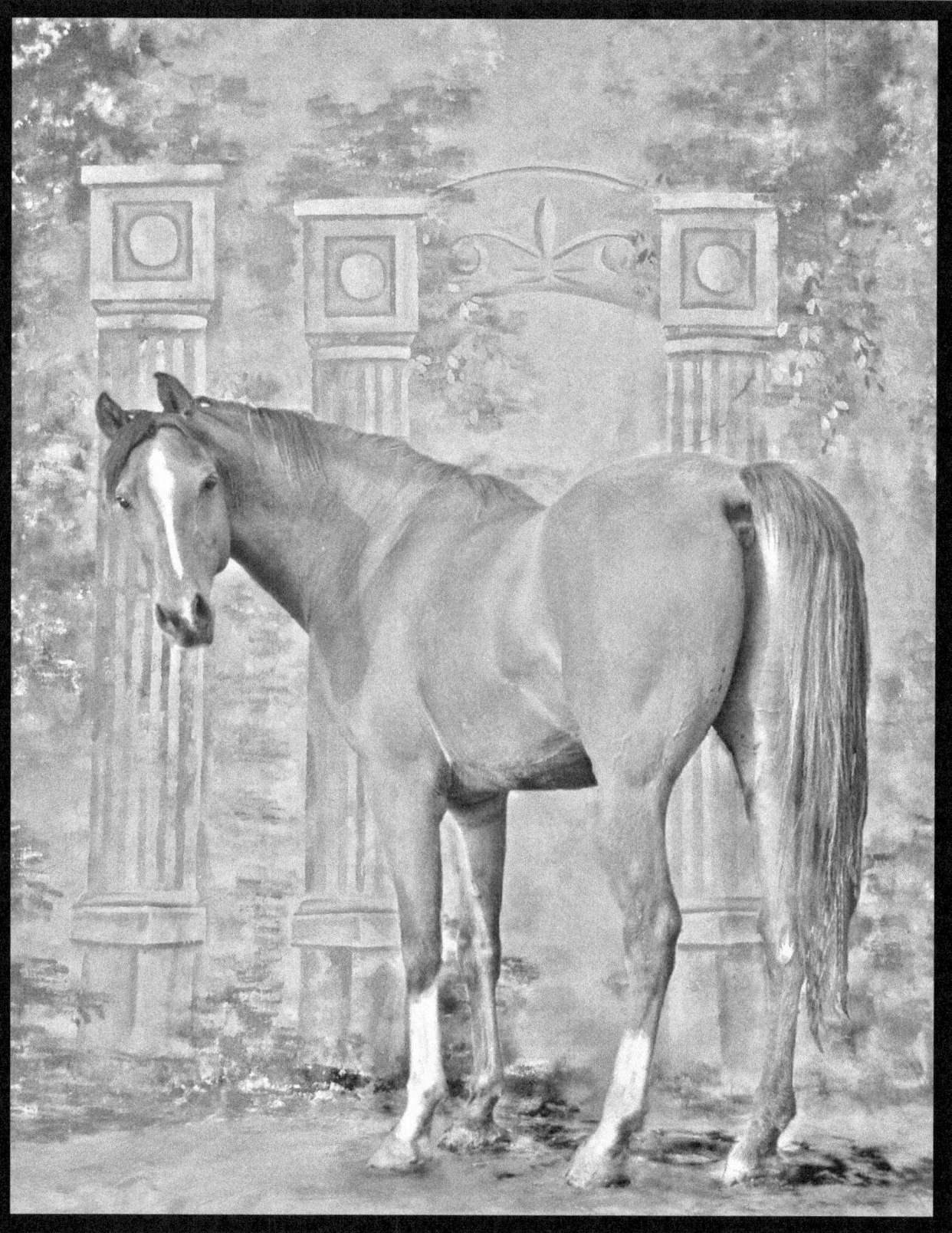

Coloring Book for Adults

Horses Lovers

By

Engy Khalil

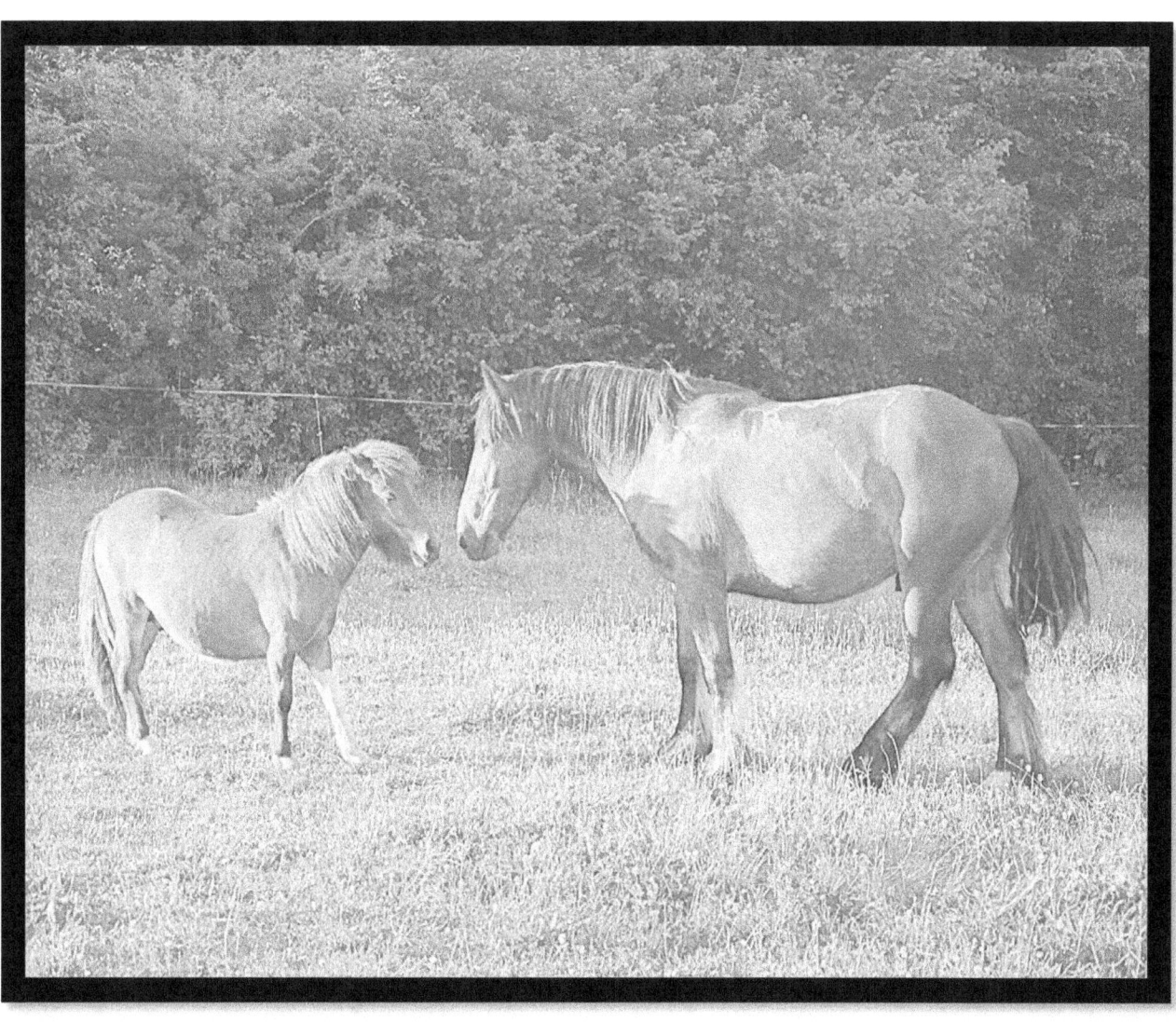

Coloring Book for Adults

Horses Lovers

By

Engy Khalil

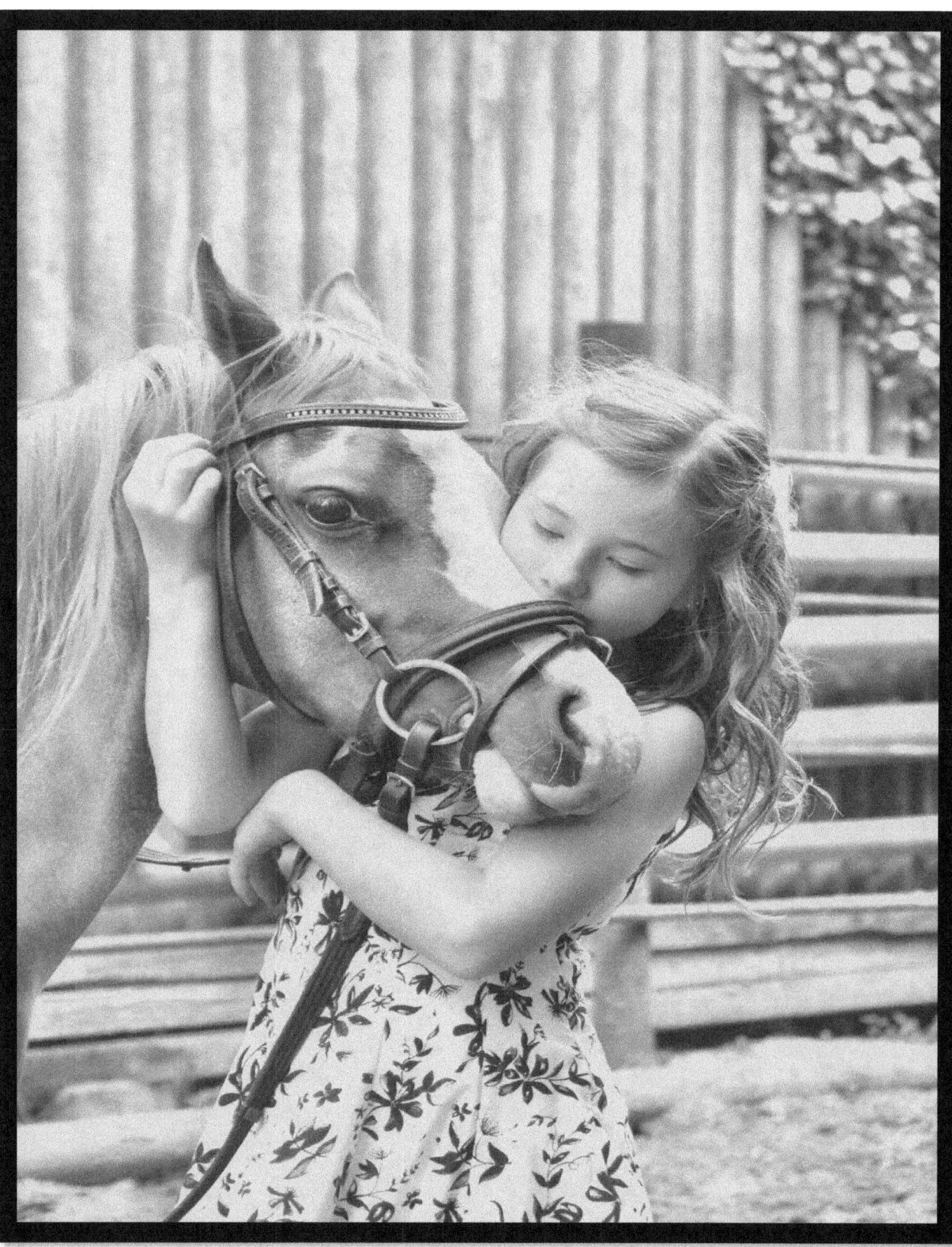

Coloring Book for Adults

Horses Lovers

By

Engy Khalil

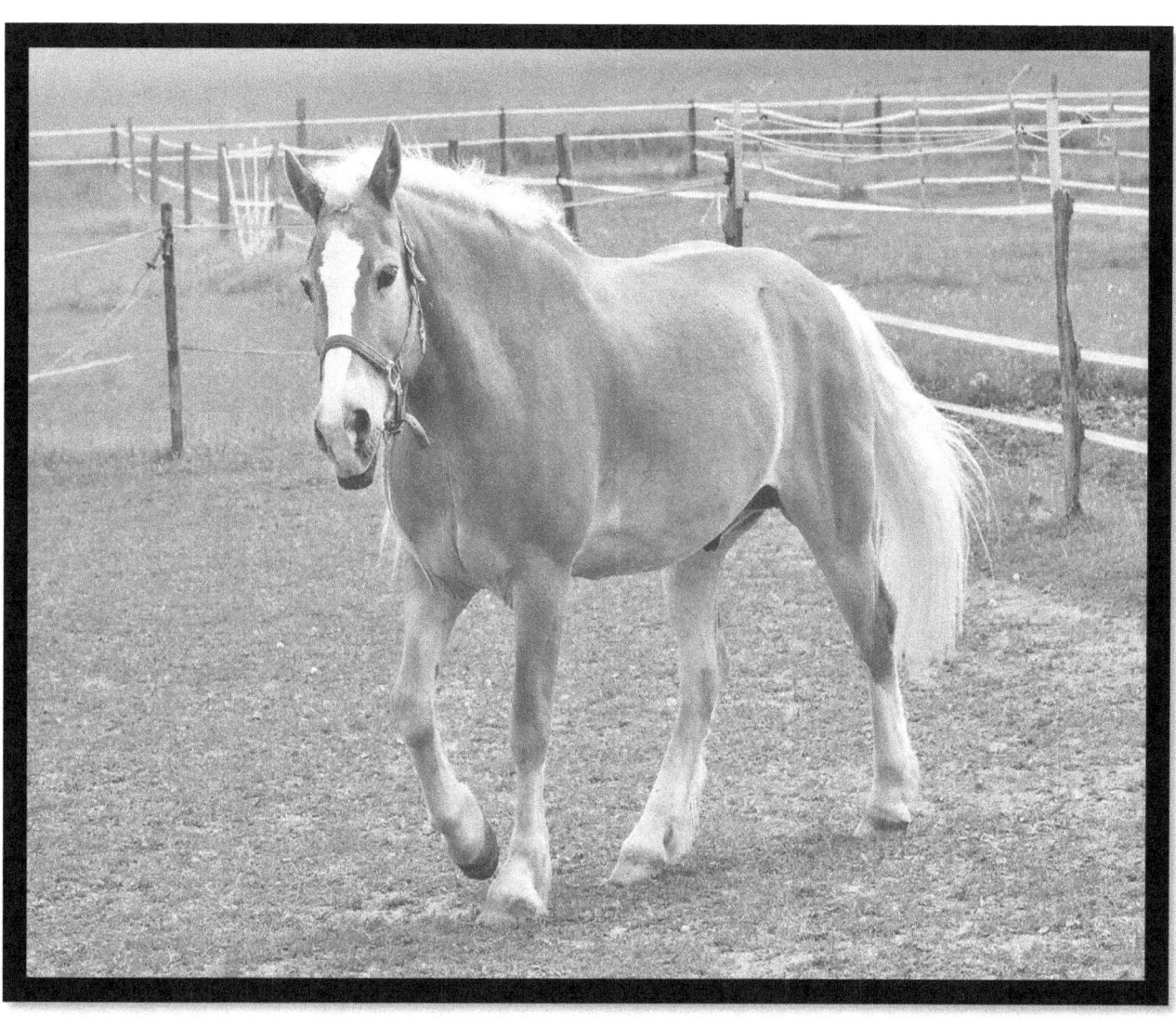

Coloring Book for Adults

Horses Lovers

By

Engy Khalil

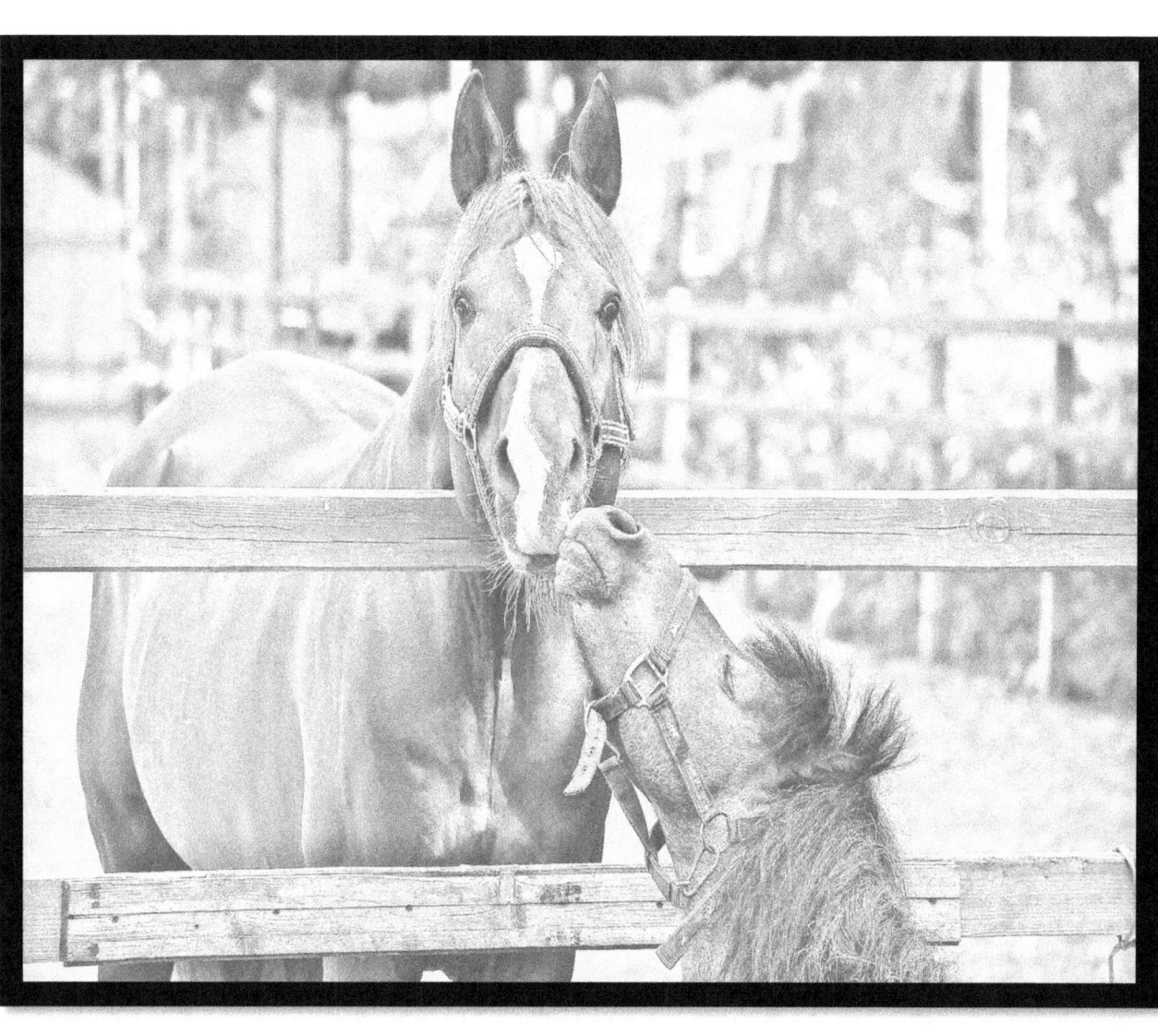

Coloring Book for Adults

Horses Lovers

By

Engy Khalil

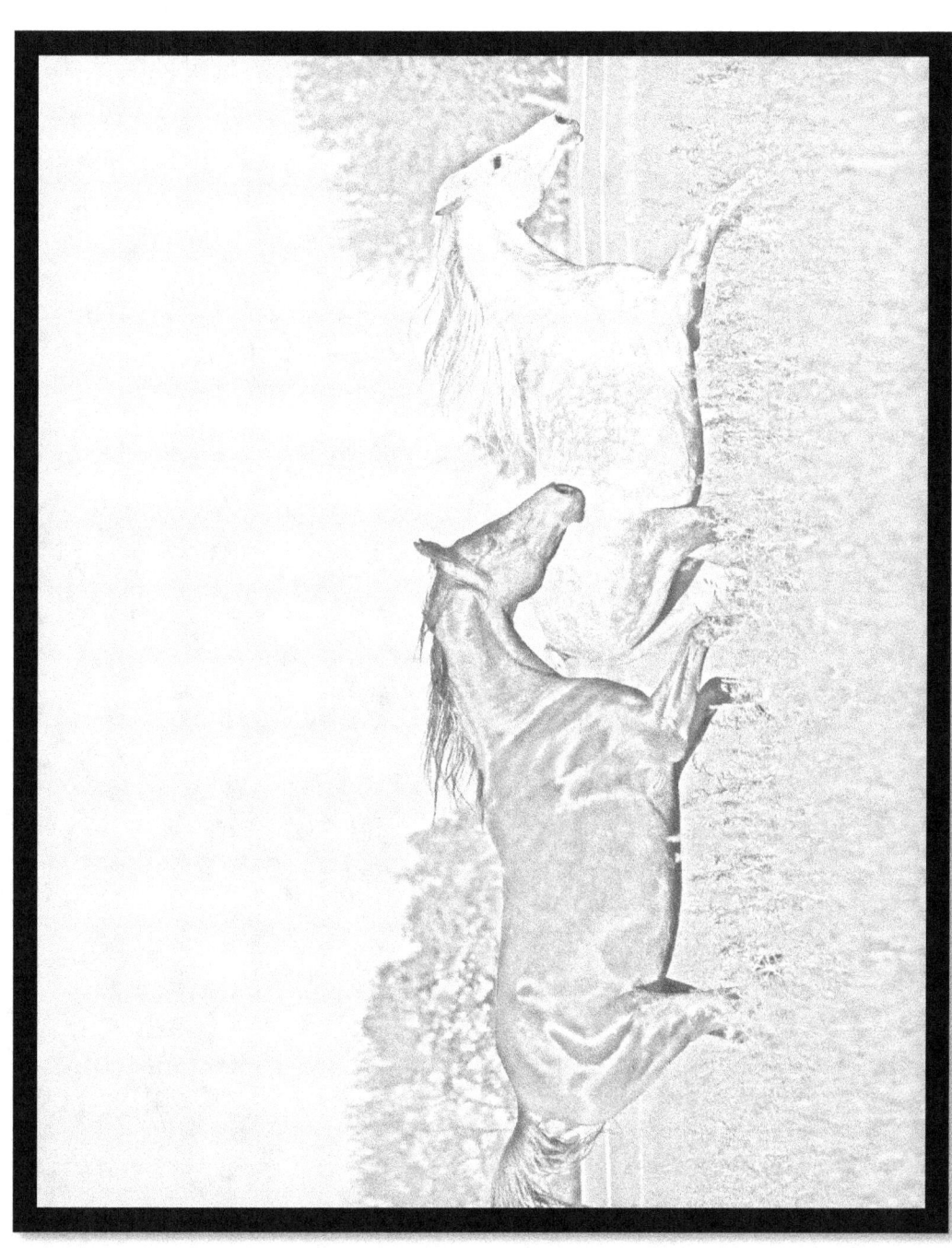

Coloring Book for Adults

Horses Lovers

By

Engy Khalil

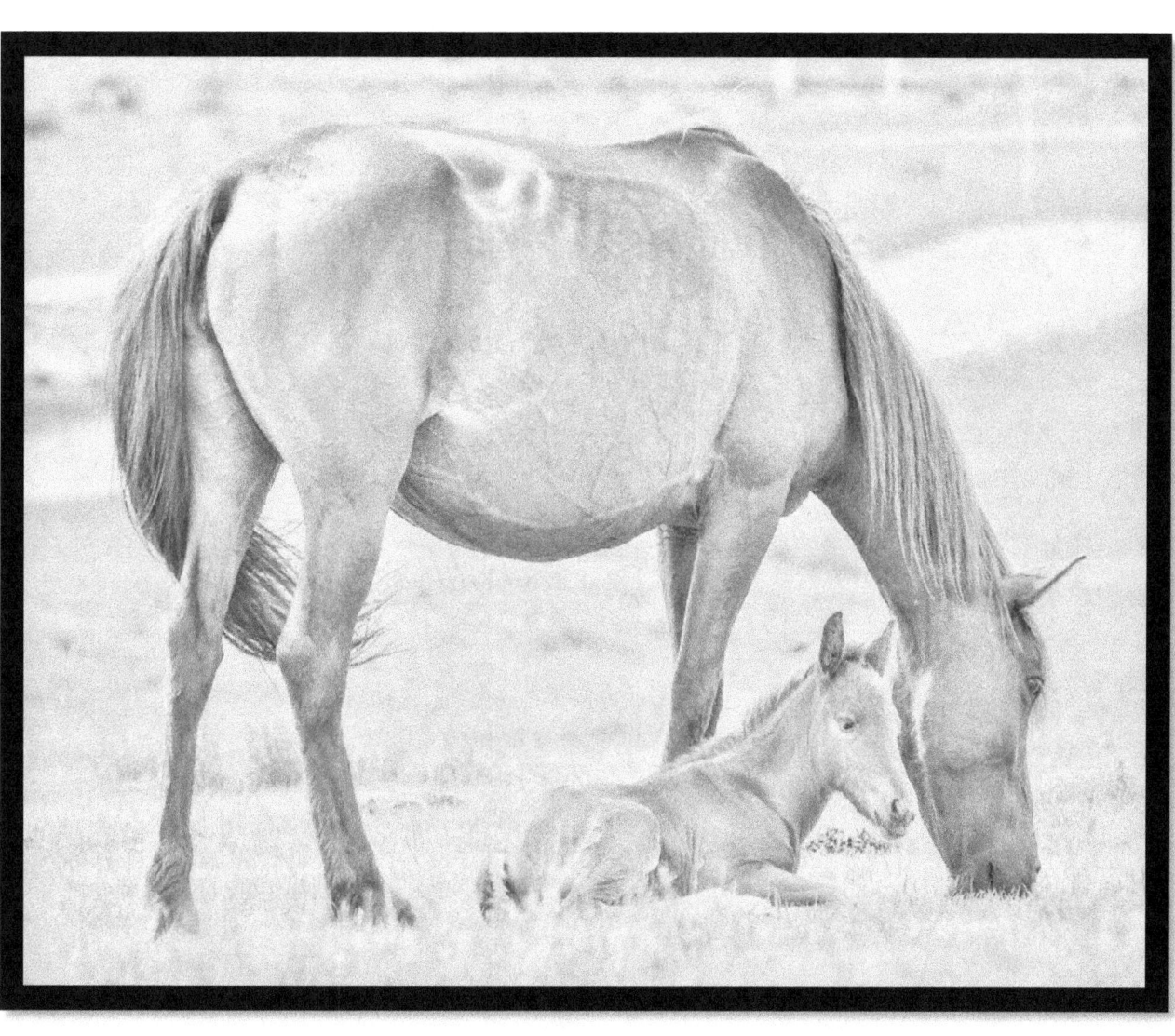

Coloring Book for Adults

Horses Lovers

By

Engy Khalil

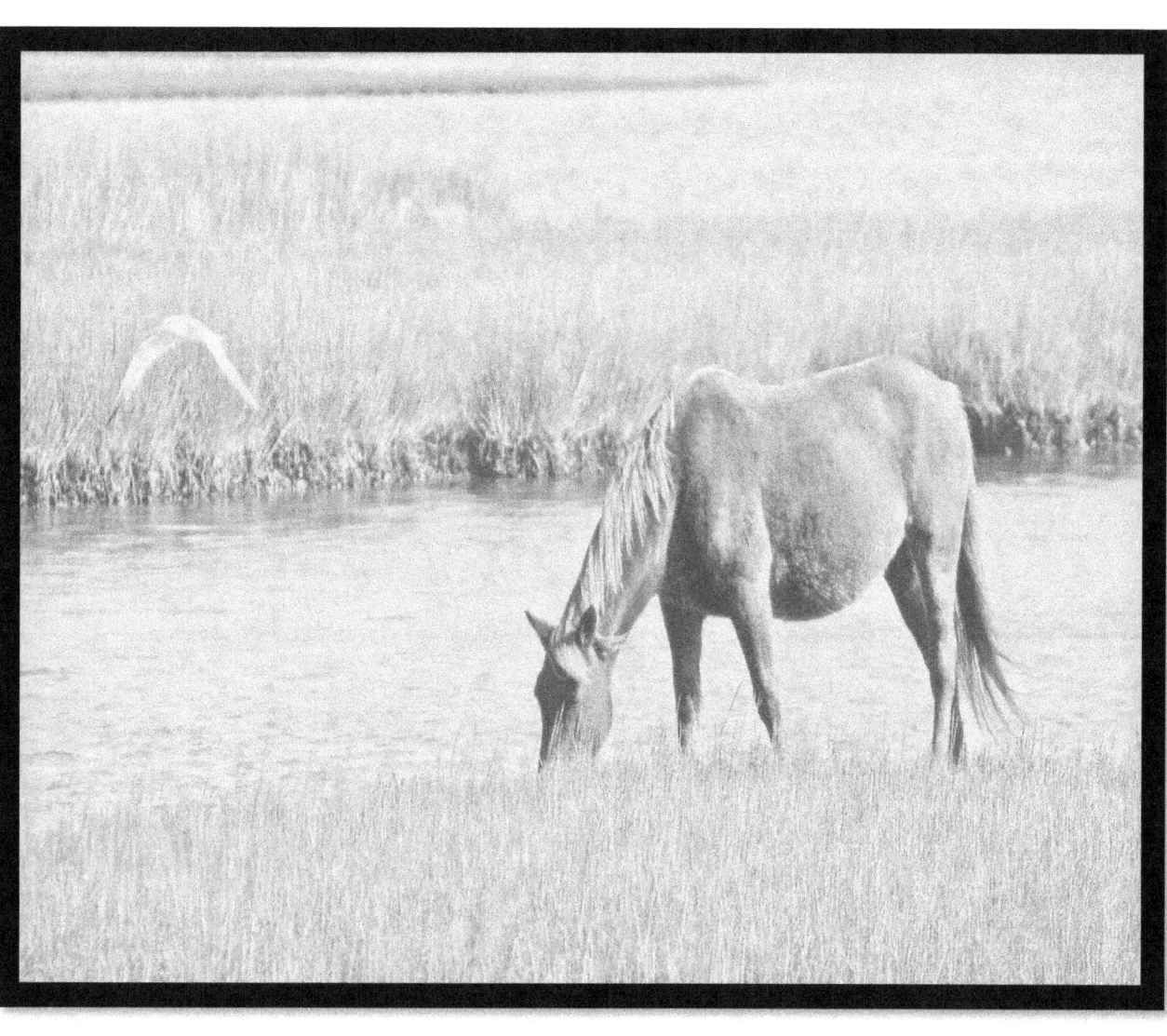

Coloring Book for Adults

Horses Lovers

By

Engy Khalil

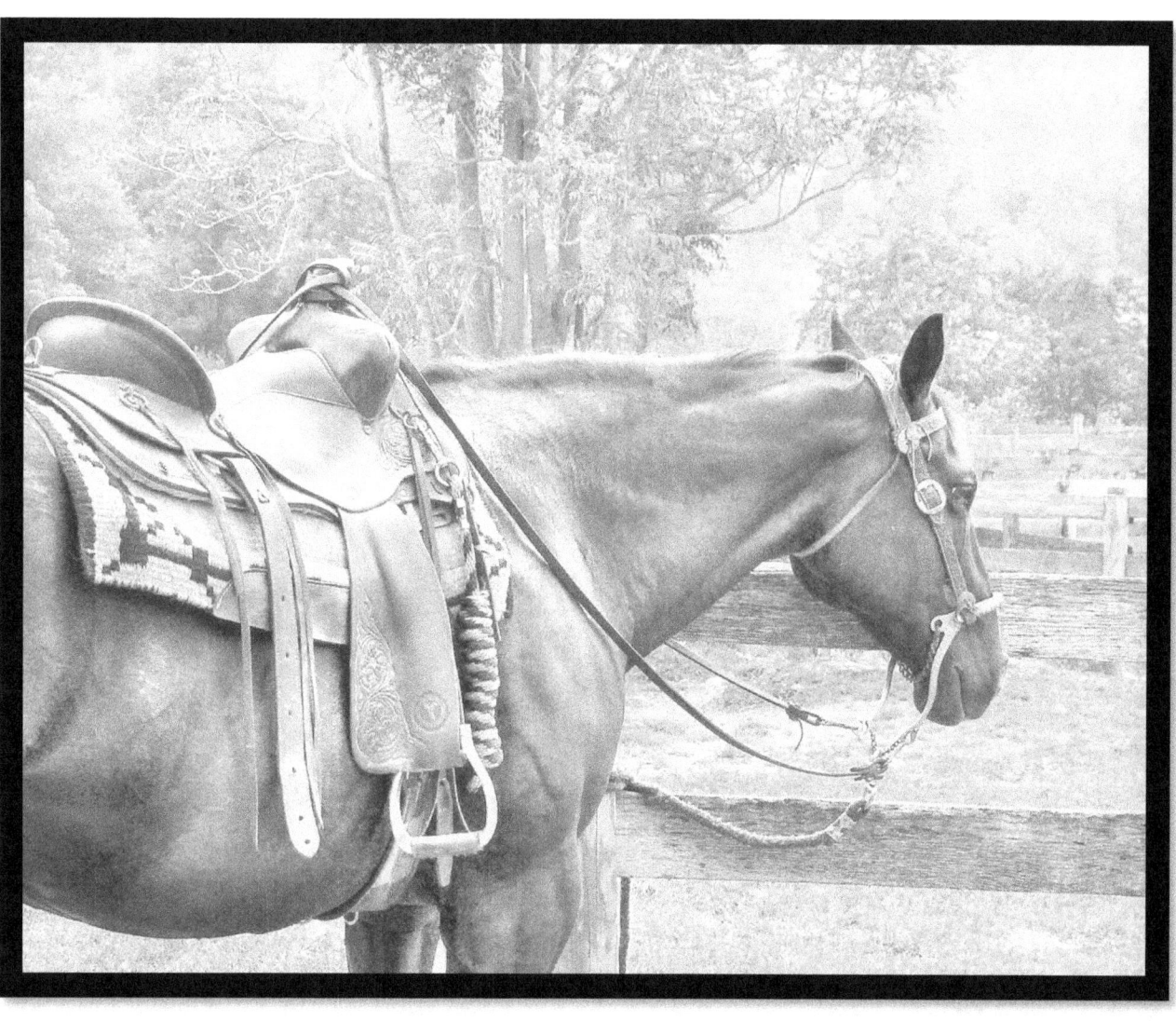

Coloring Book for Adults

Horses Lovers

By

Engy Khalil

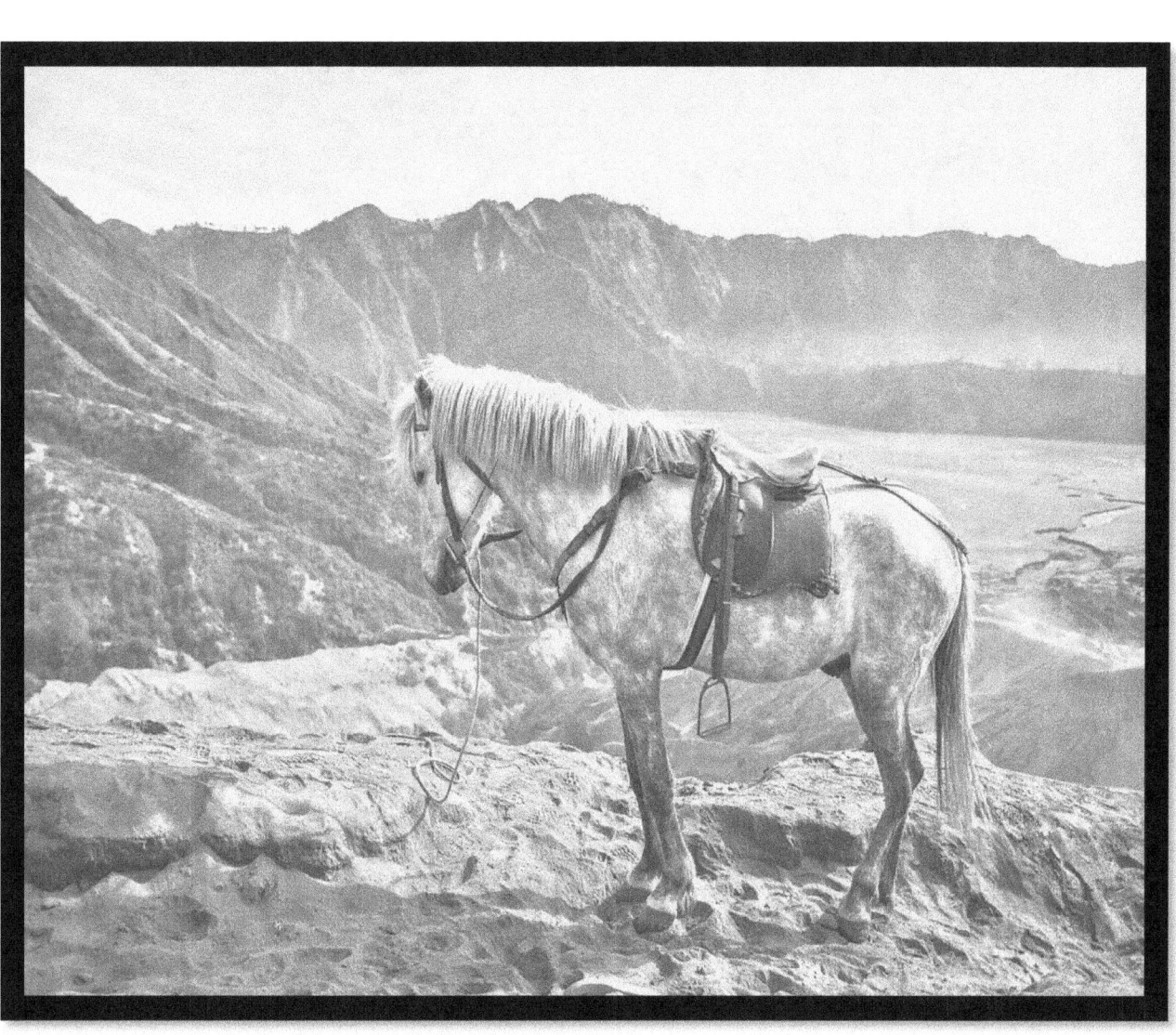

Coloring Book for Adults

Horses Lovers

By

Engy Khalil

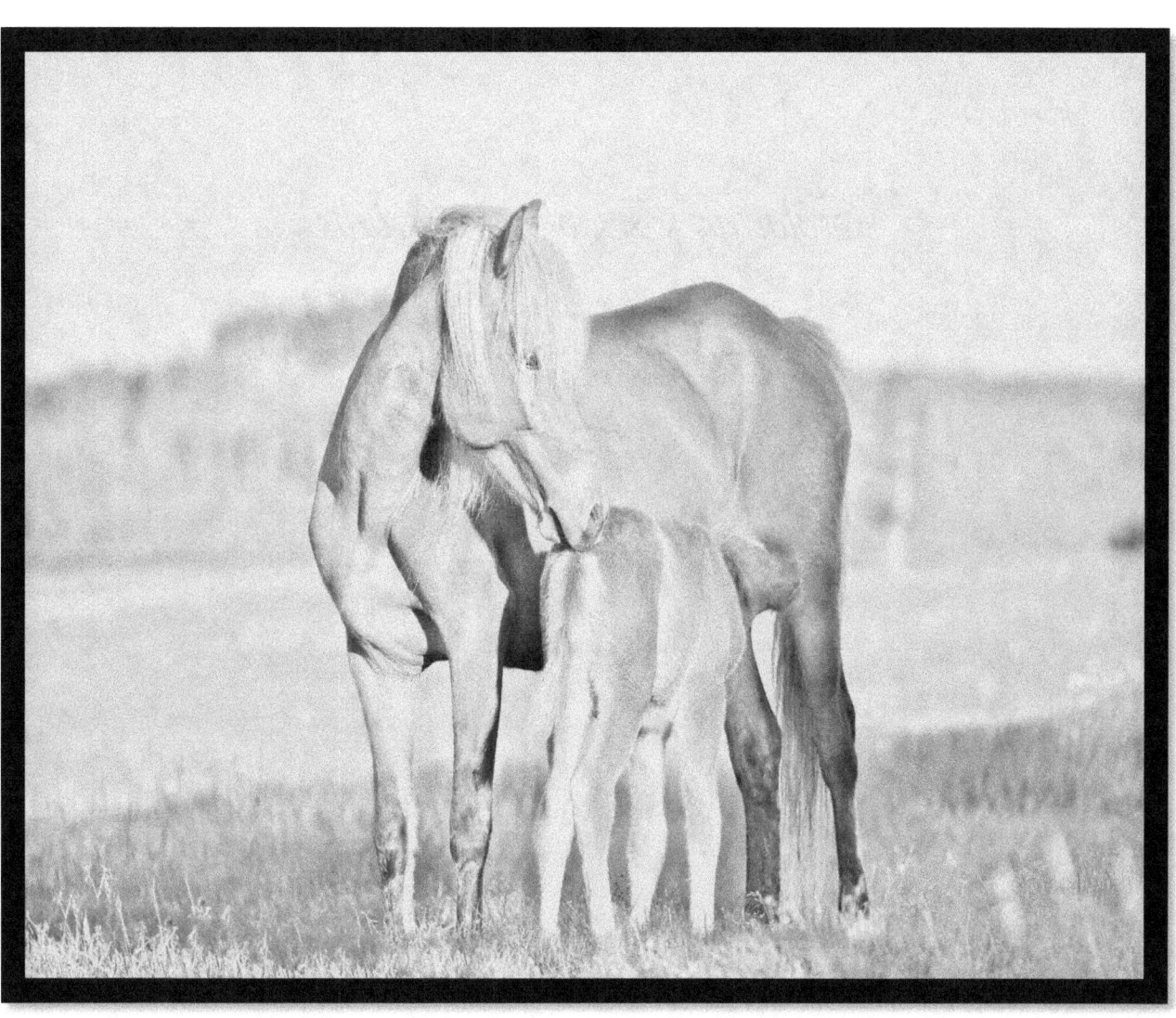

Coloring Book for Adults

Horses Lovers

By

Engy Khalil

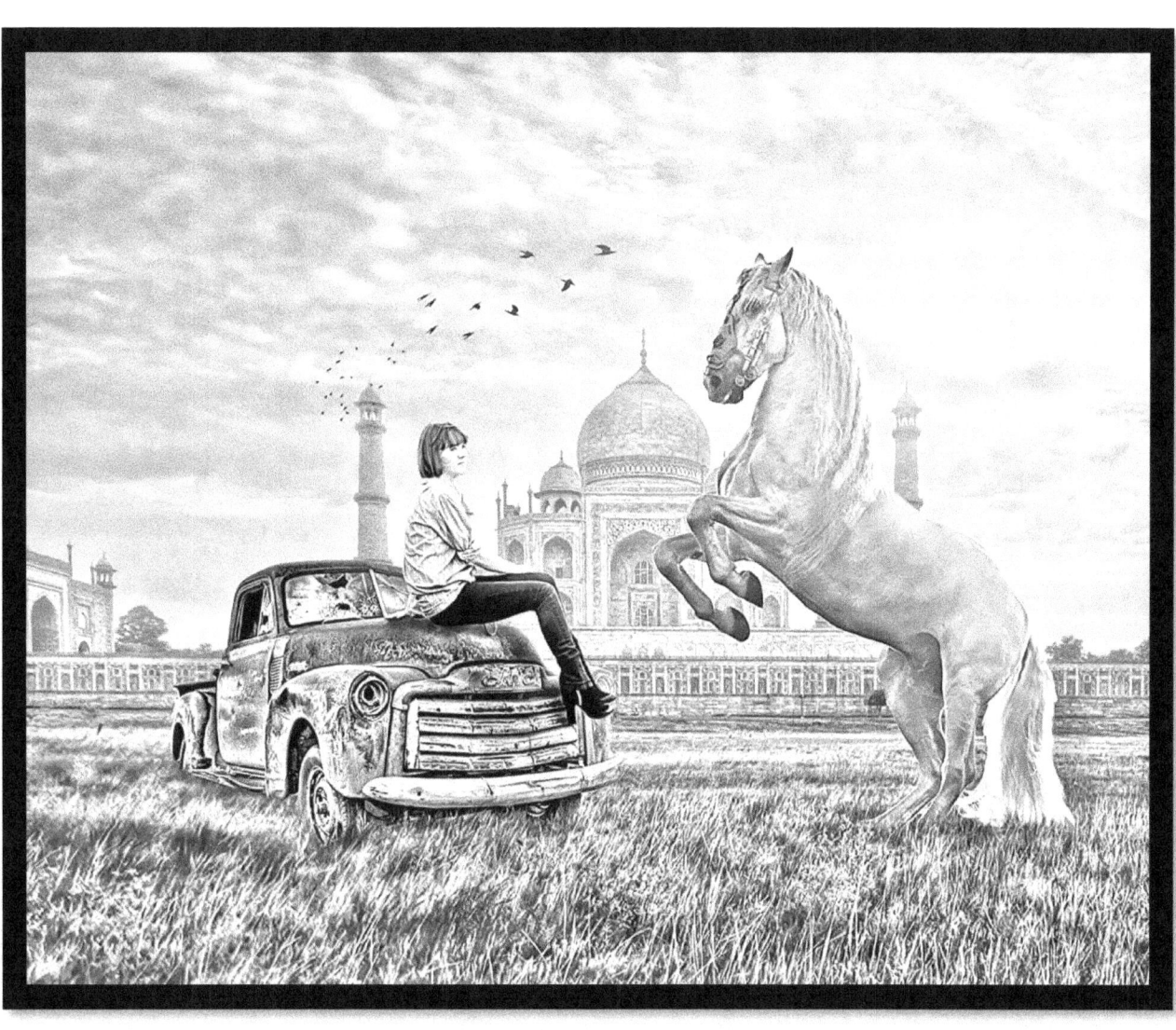

Coloring Book for Adults

Horses Lovers

By

Engy Khalil

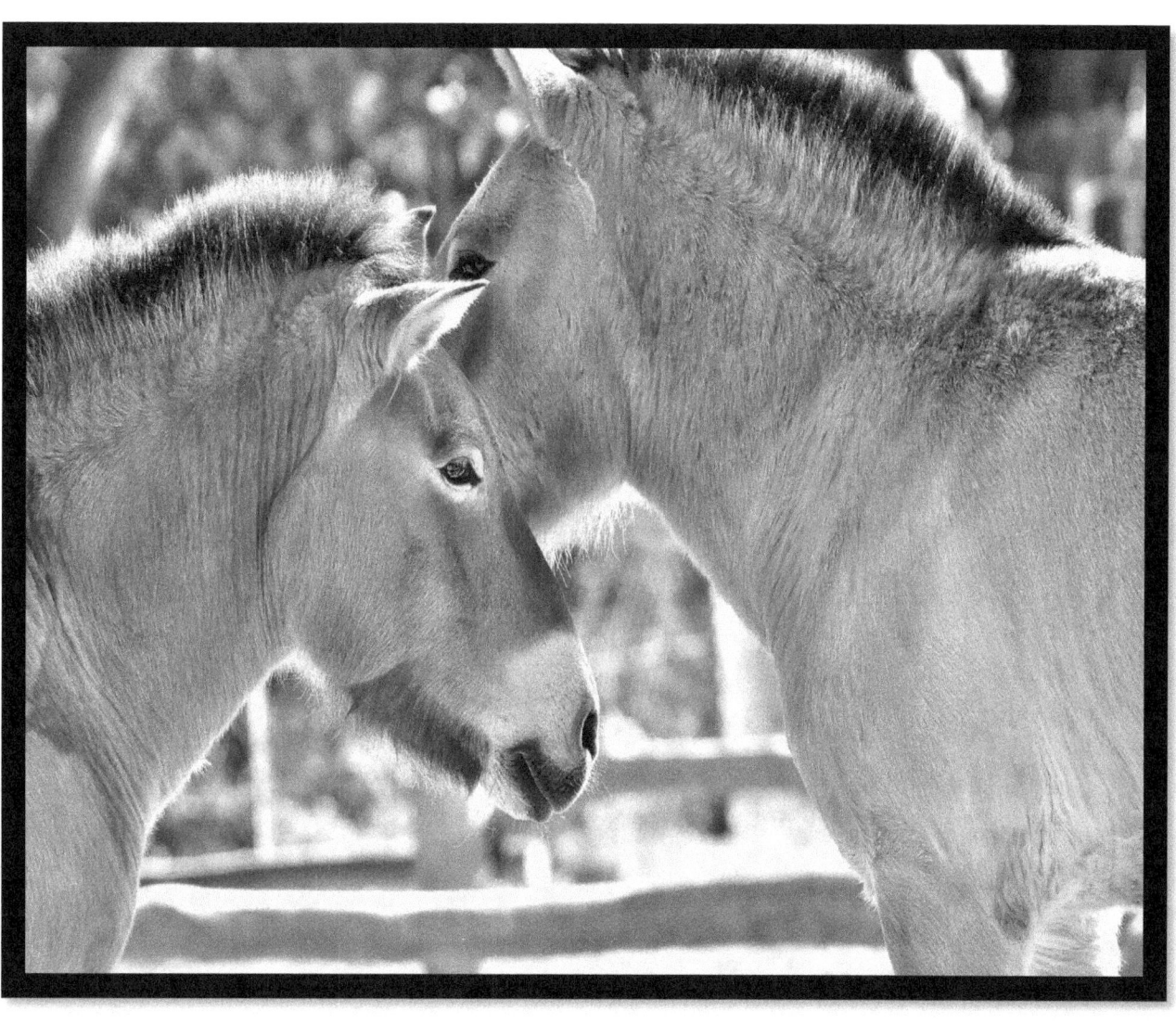

Coloring Book for Adults

Horses Lovers

By

Engy Khalil

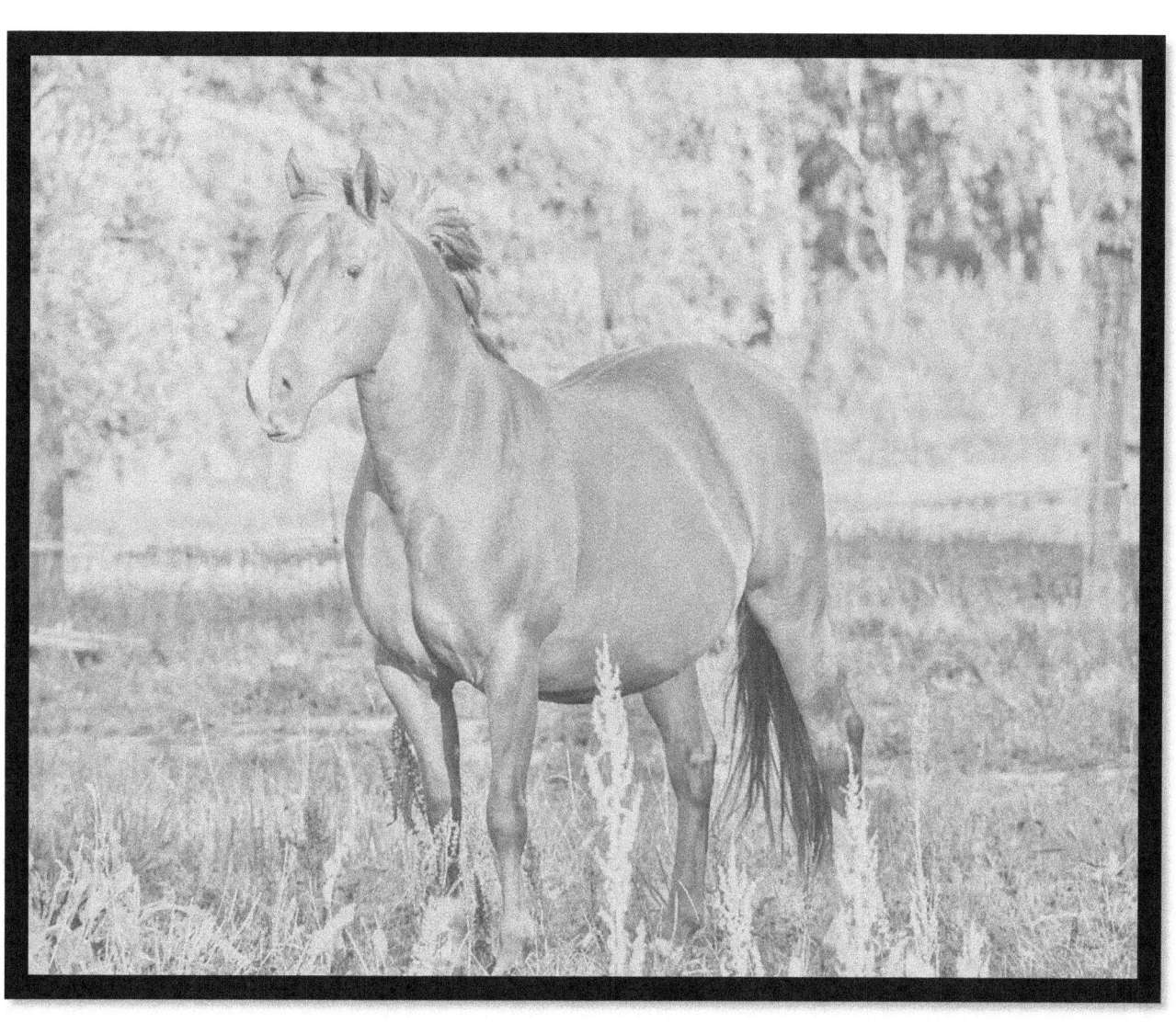

Coloring Book for Adults

Horses Lovers

By

Engy Khalil

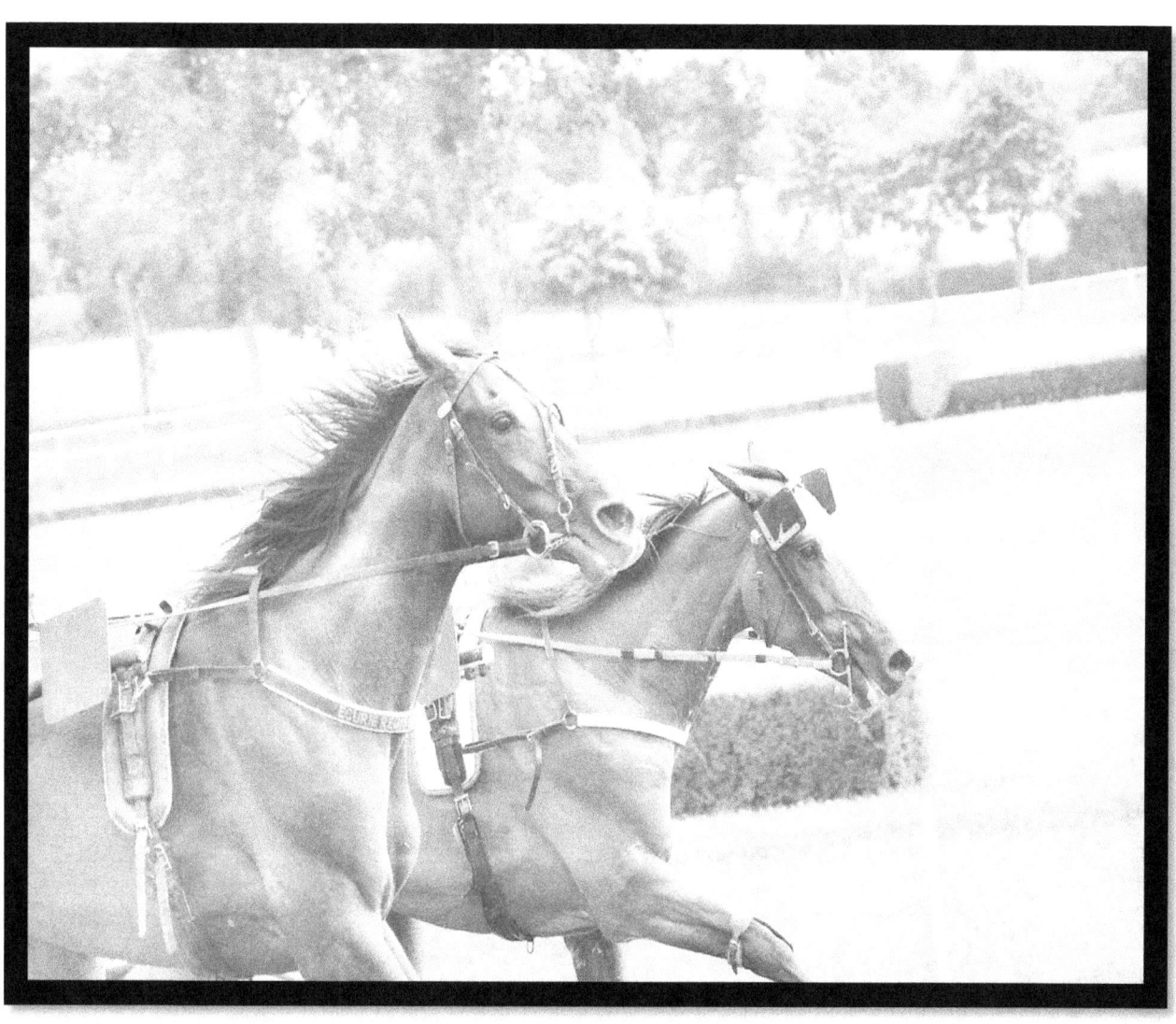

Coloring Book for Adults

Horses Lovers

By

Engy Khalil

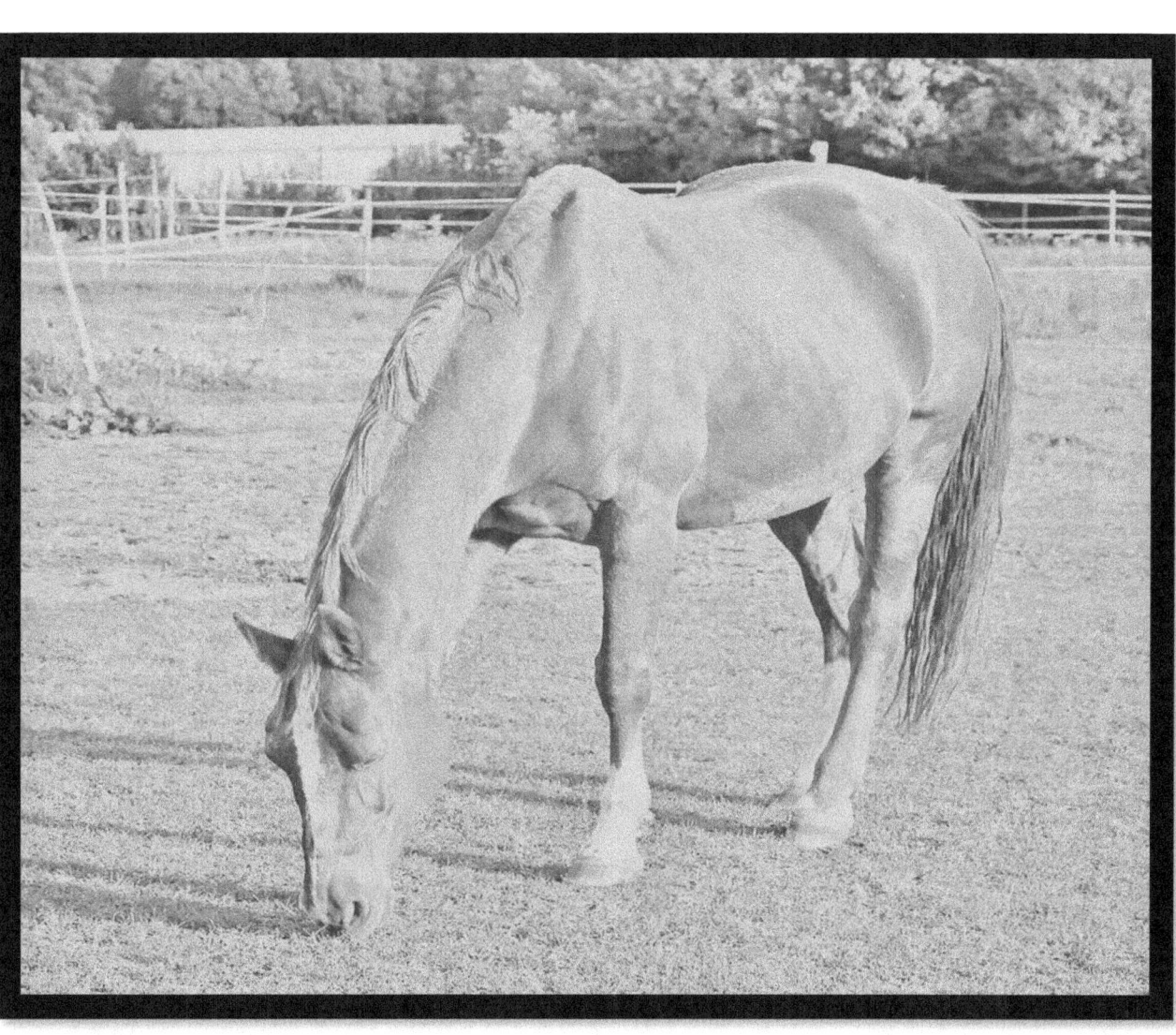

Coloring Book for Adults

Horses Lovers

By

Engy Khalil

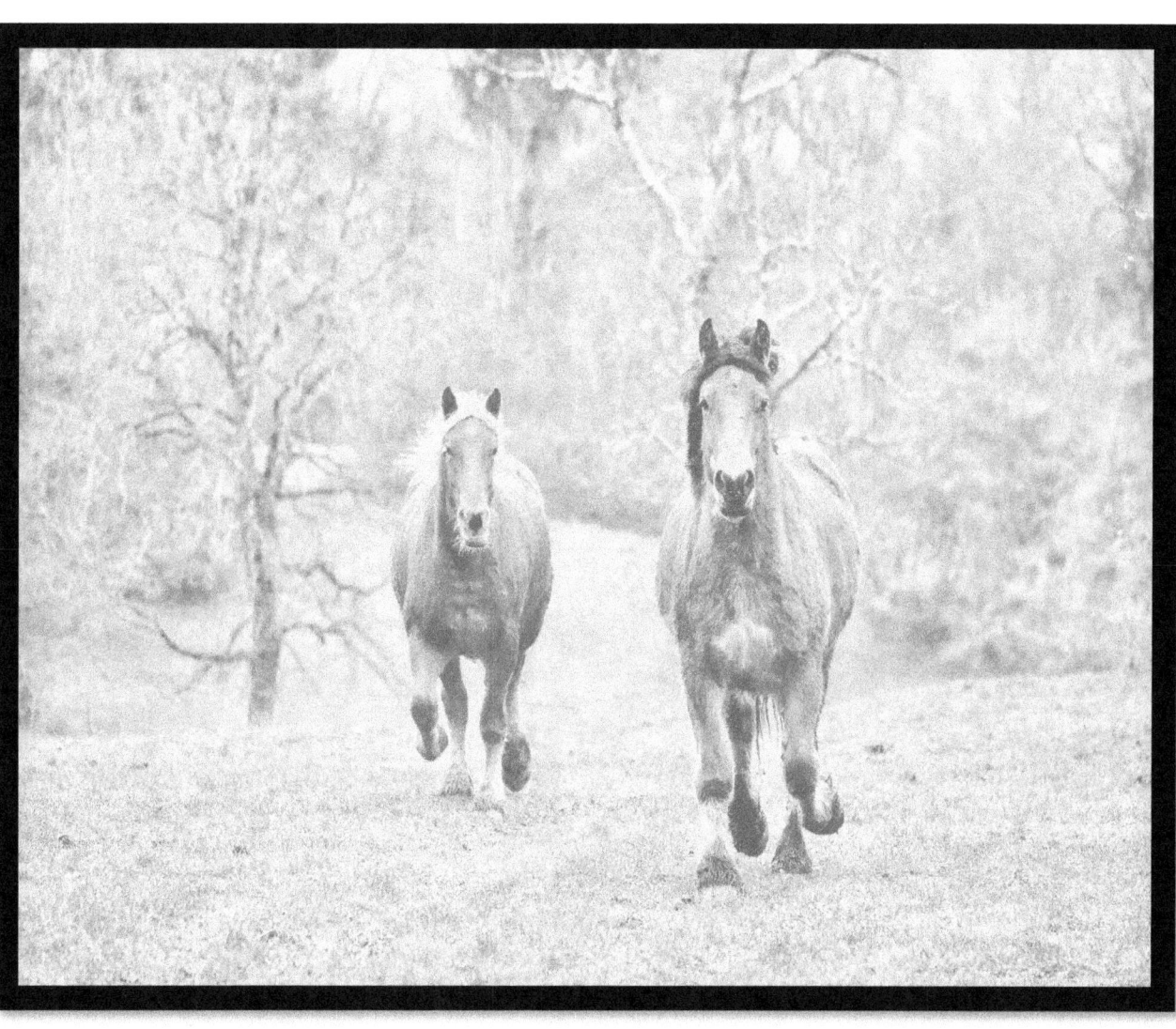

Coloring Book for Adults

Horses Lovers

By

Engy Khalil

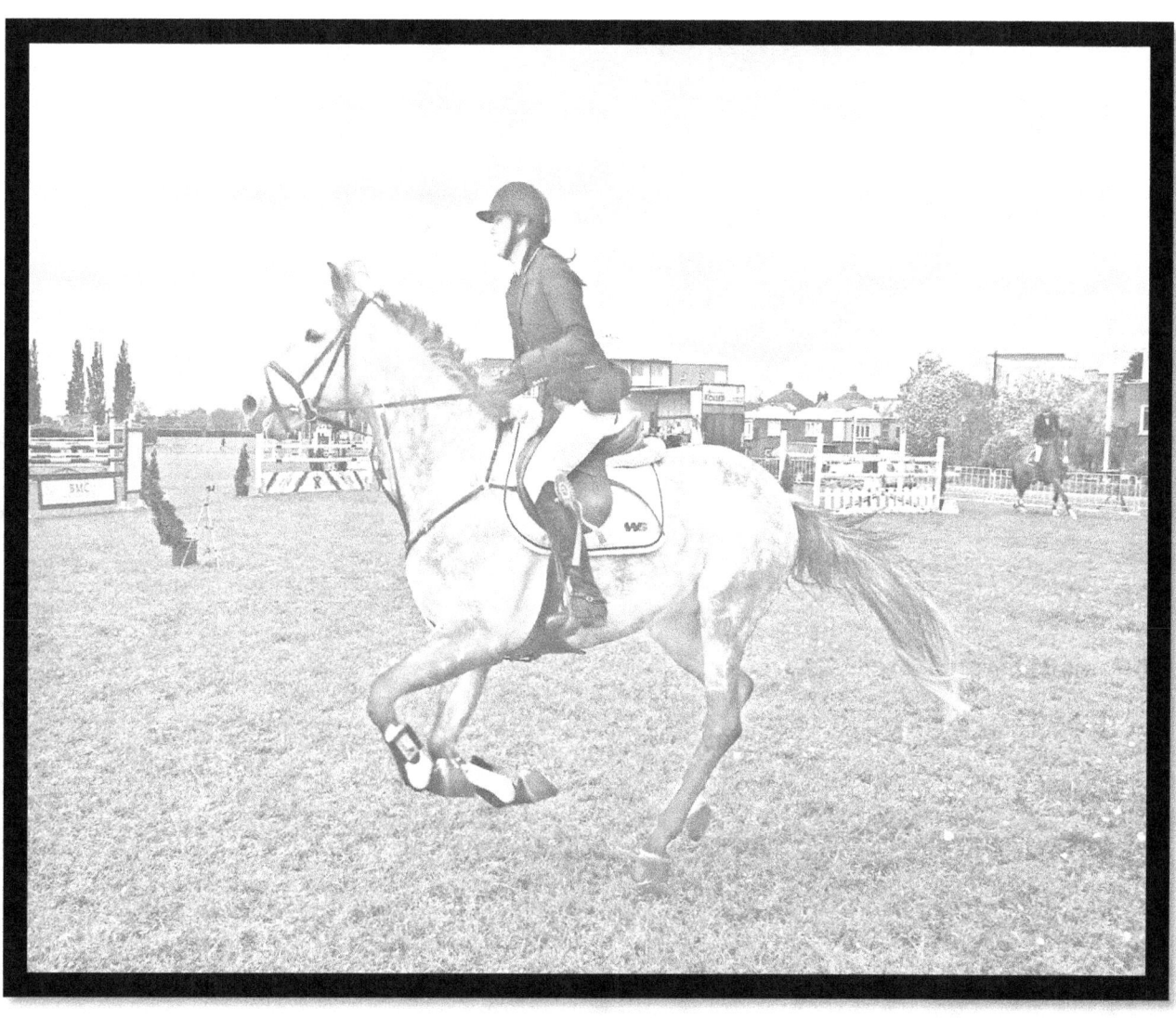

Coloring Book for Adults

Horses Lovers

By

Engy Khalil

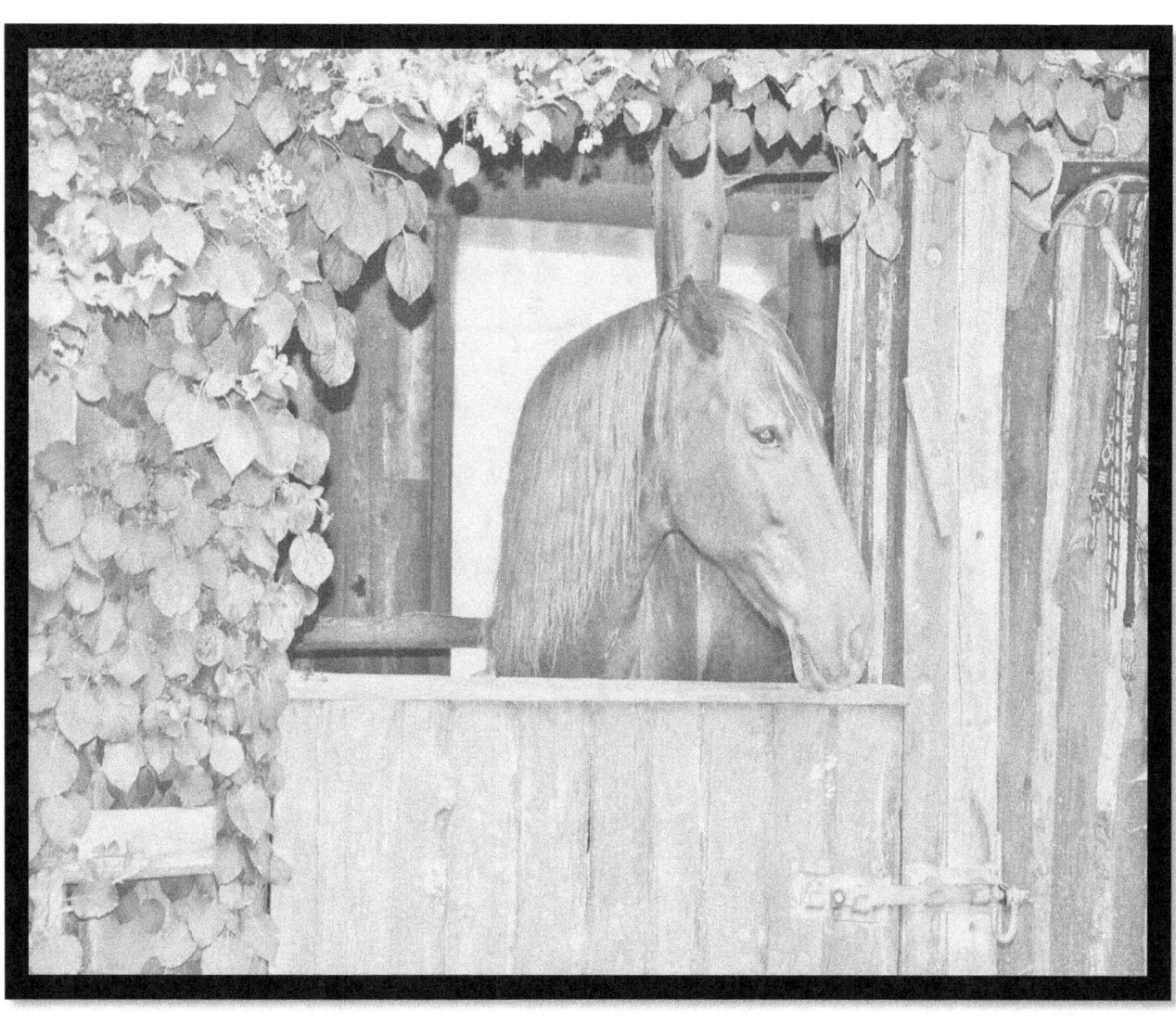

Coloring Book for Adults

Horses Lovers

By

Engy Khalil

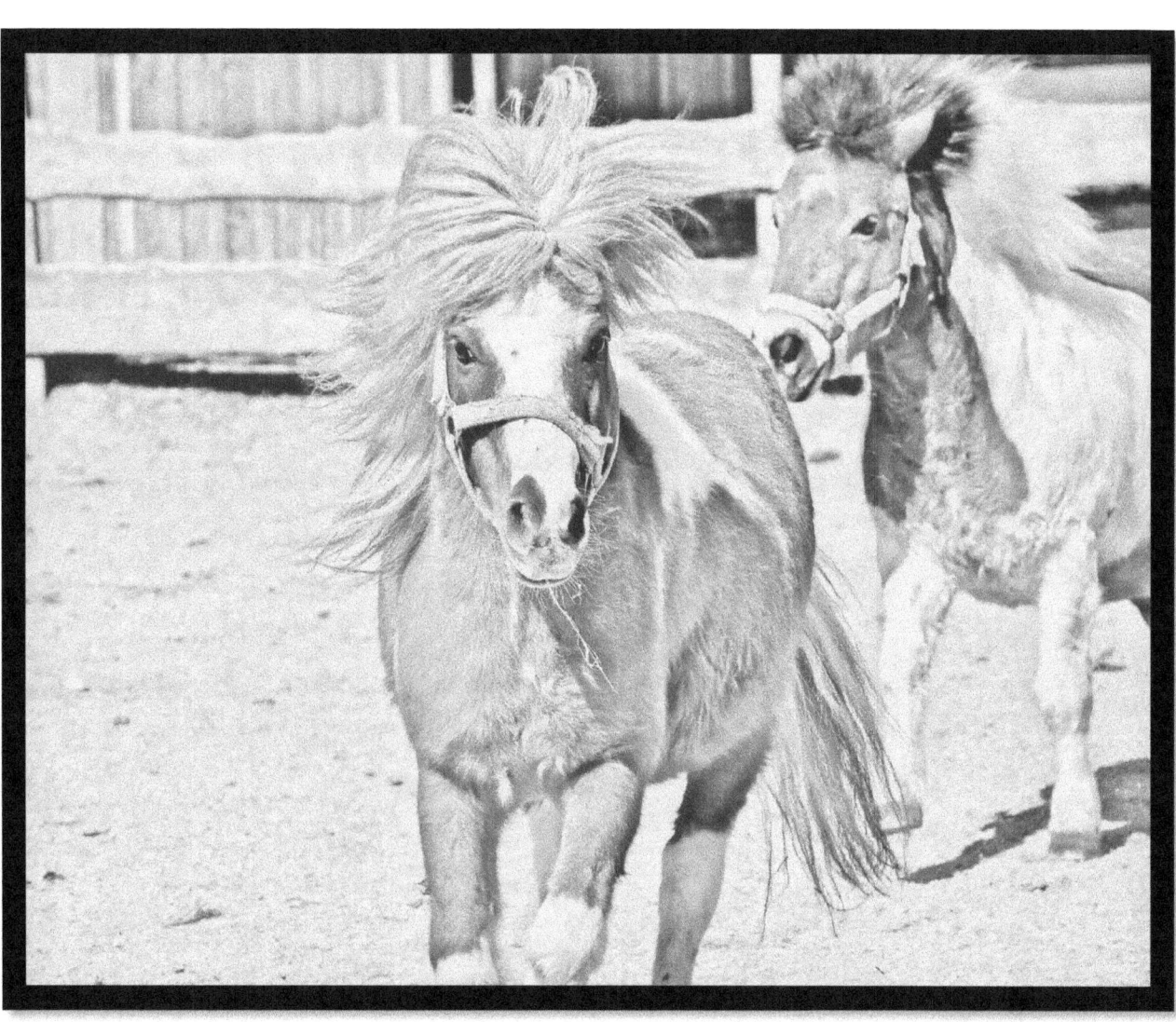

Coloring Book for Adults

Horses Lovers

By

Engy Khalil

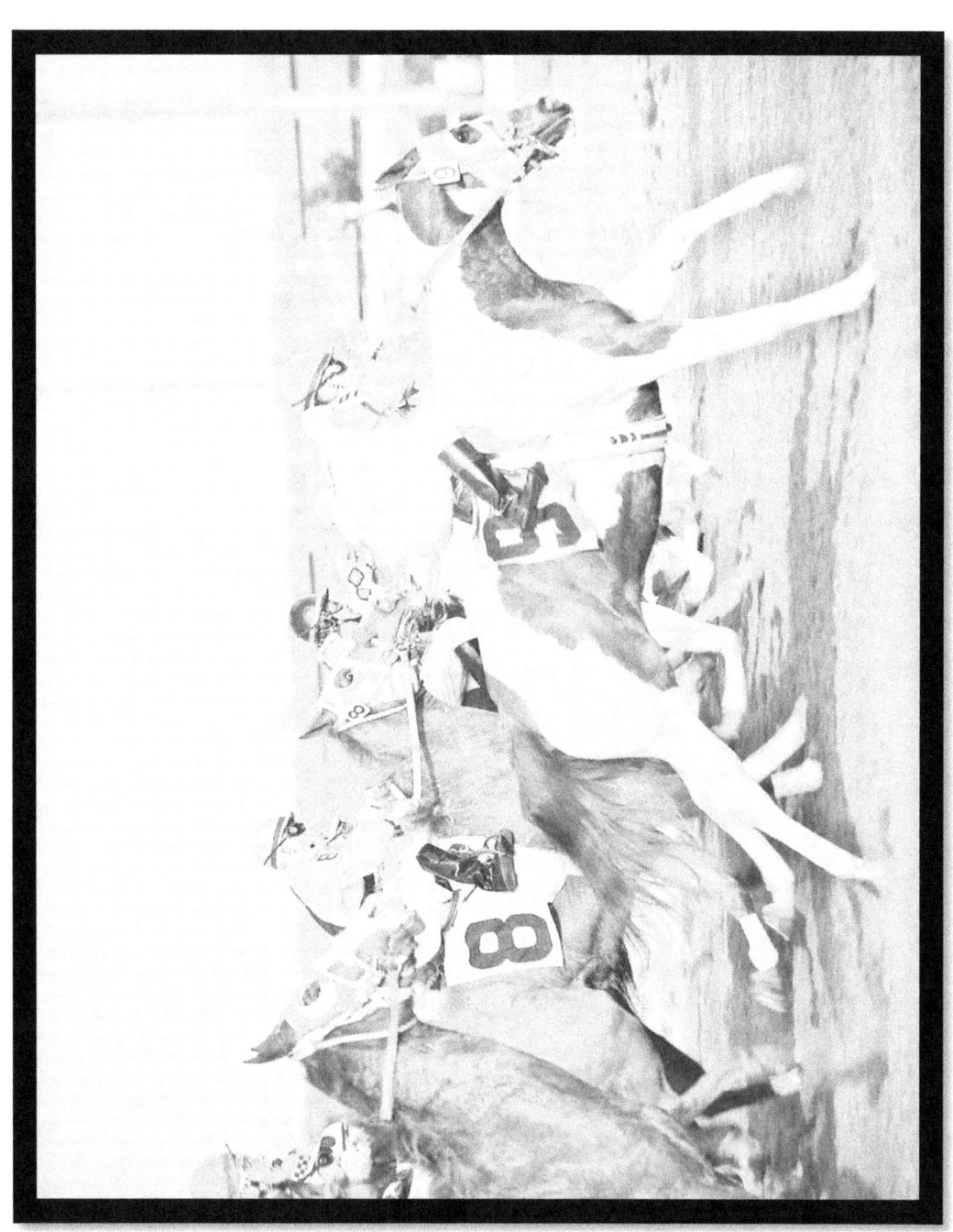

Coloring Book for Adults

Horses Lovers

By

Engy Khalil

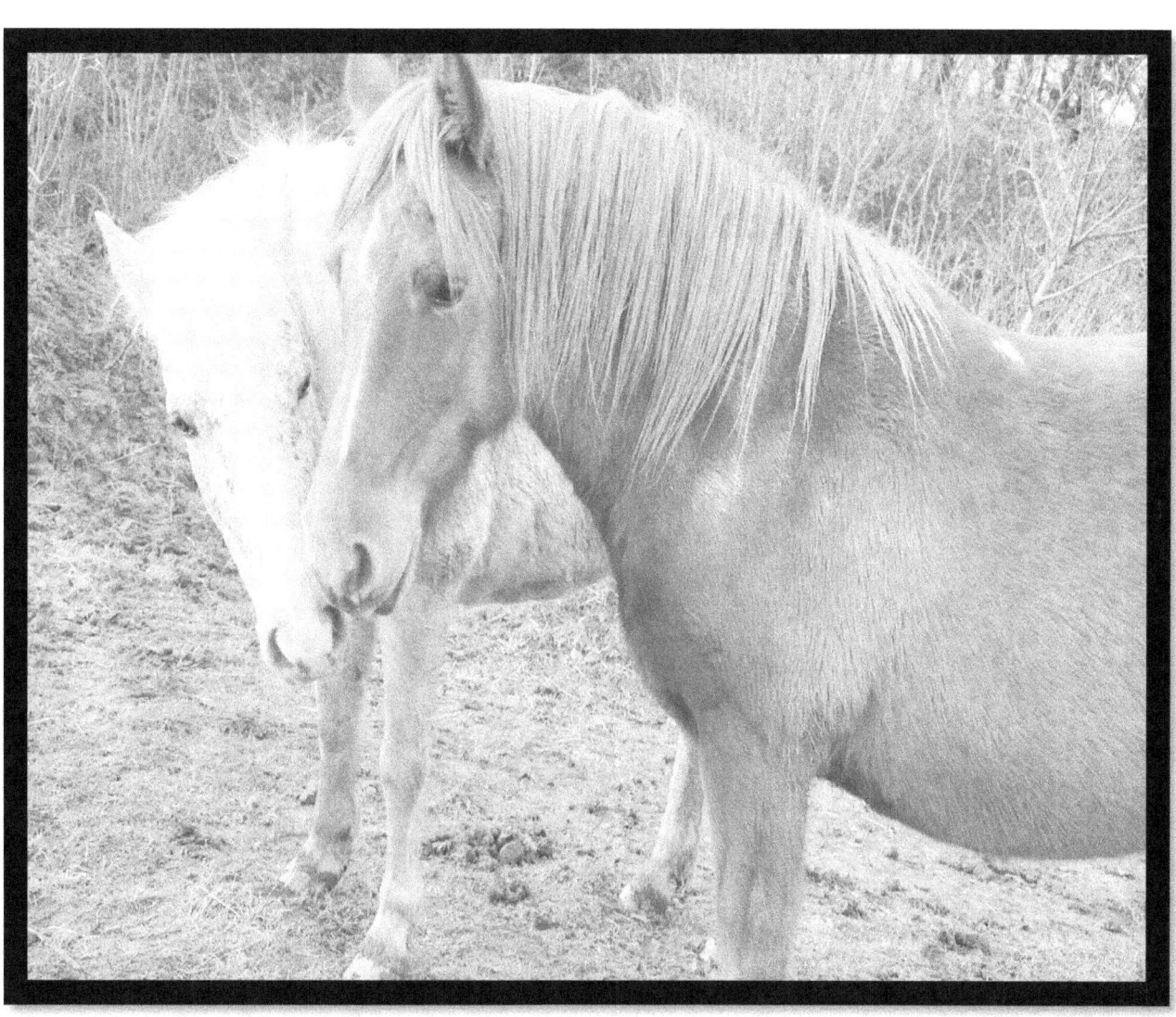

Coloring Book for Adults

Horses Lovers

By

Engy Khalil

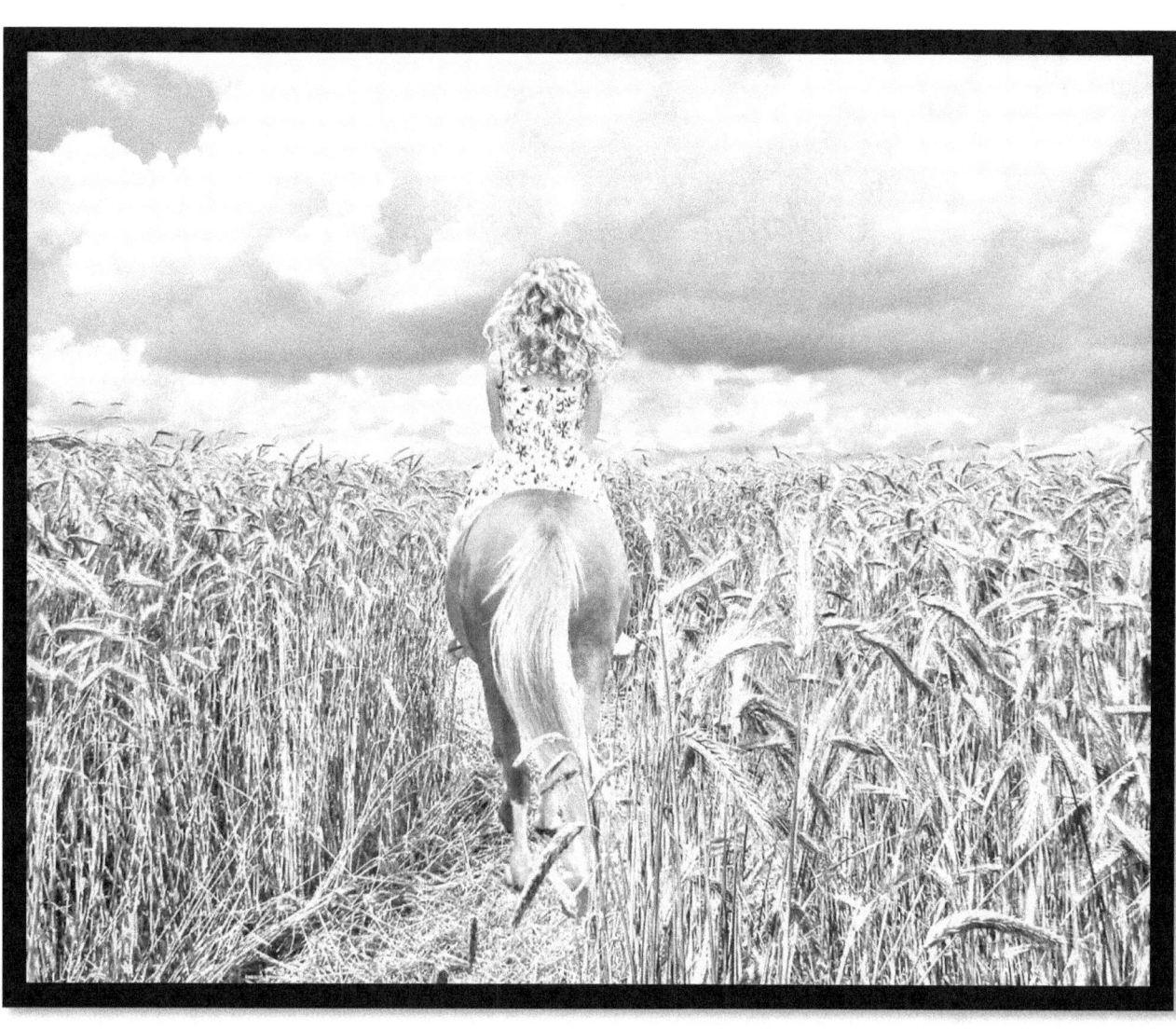

Coloring Book for Adults

Horses Lovers

By

Engy Khalil

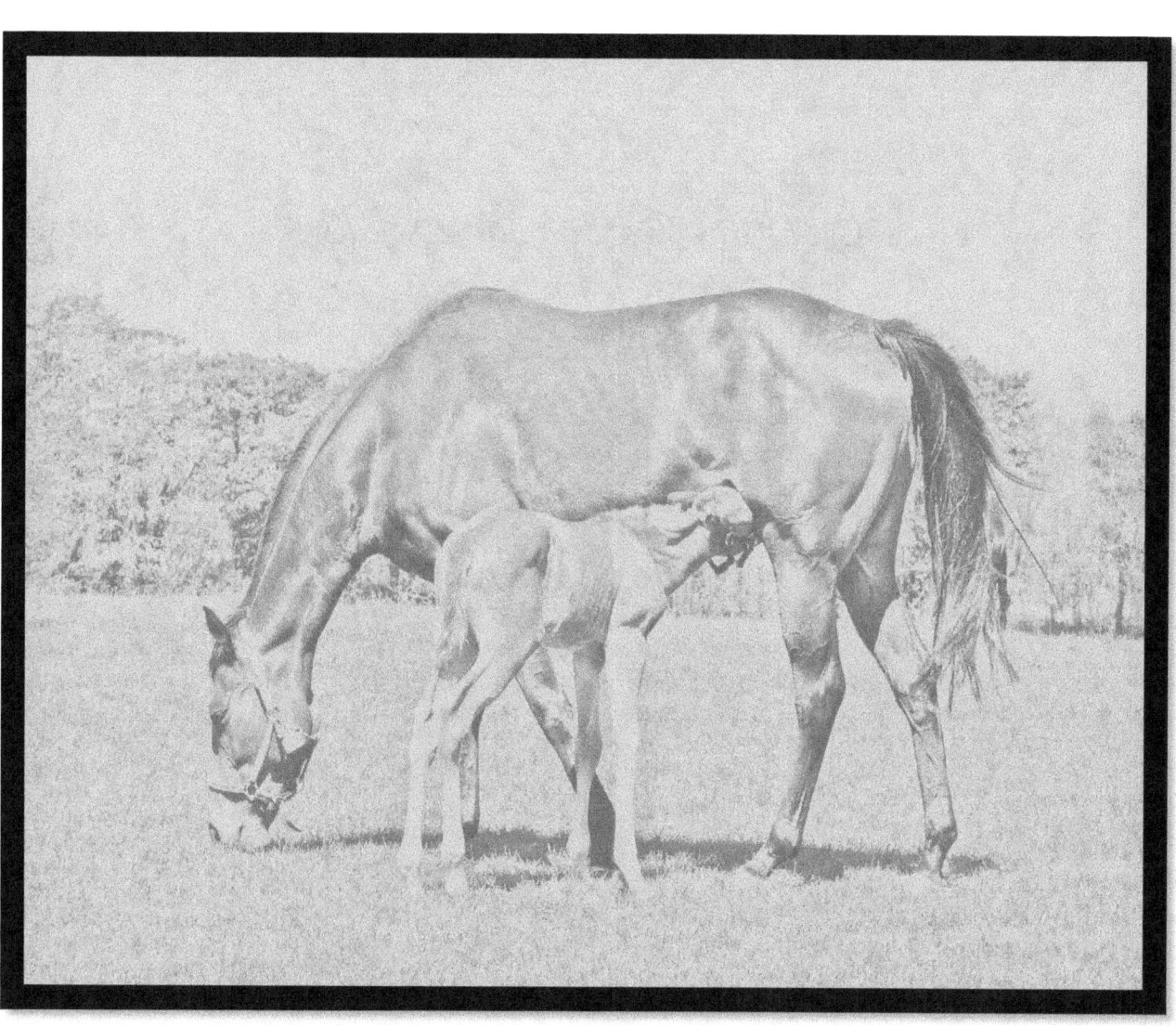

Coloring Book for Adults

Horses Lovers

By

Engy Khalil

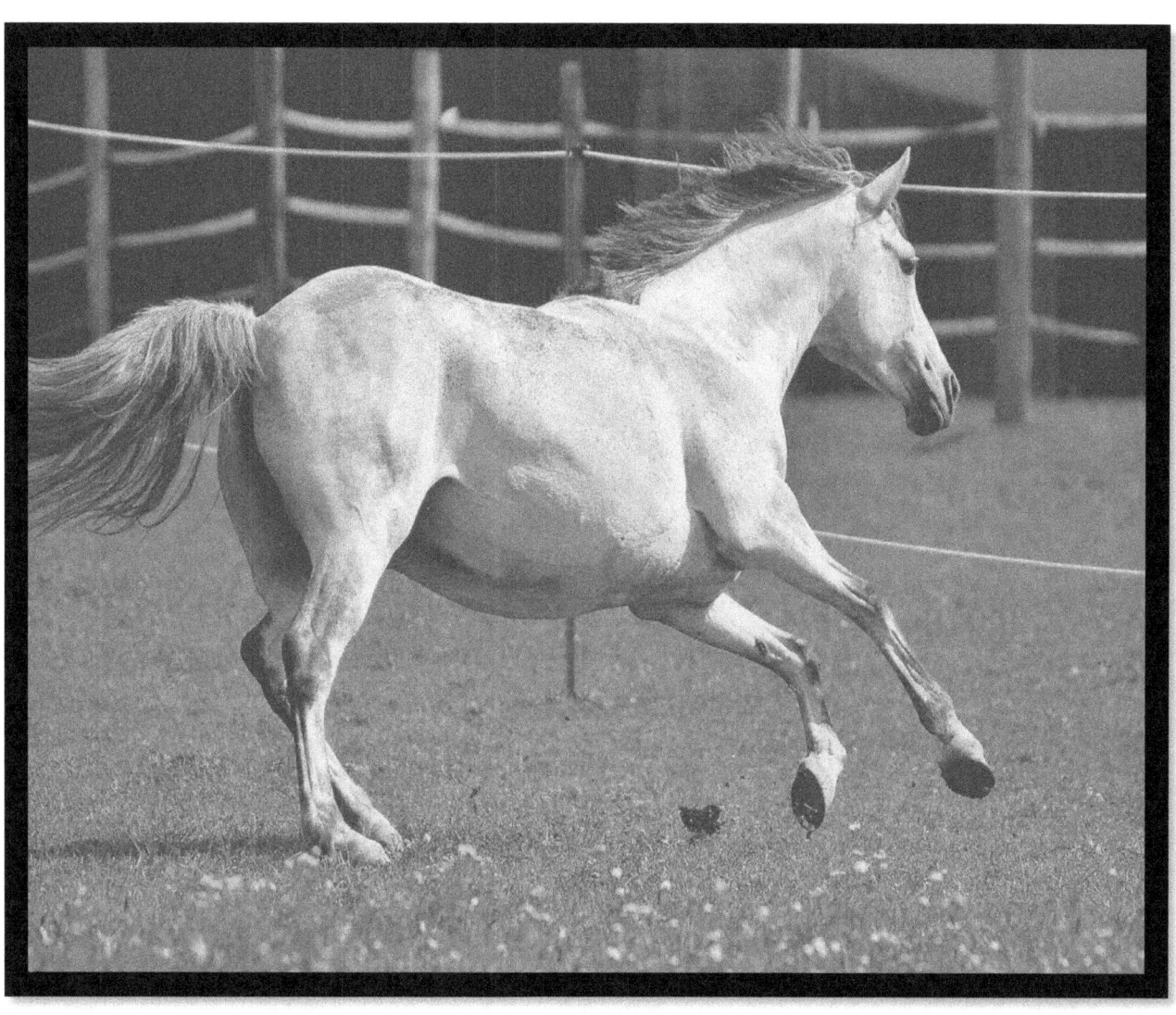

Coloring Book for Adults

Horses Lovers

By

Engy Khalil

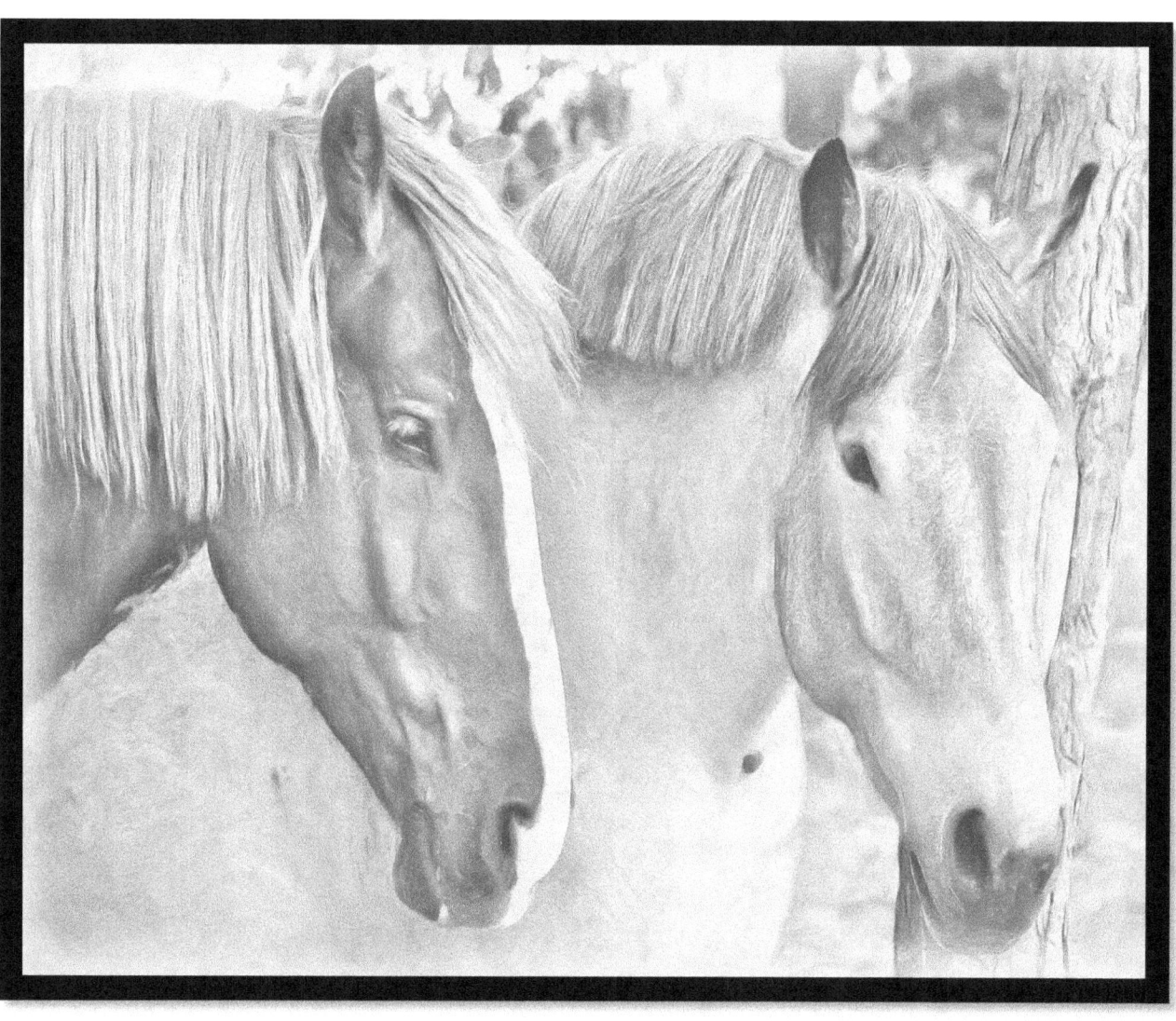

Coloring Book for Adults

Horses Lovers

By

Engy Khalil

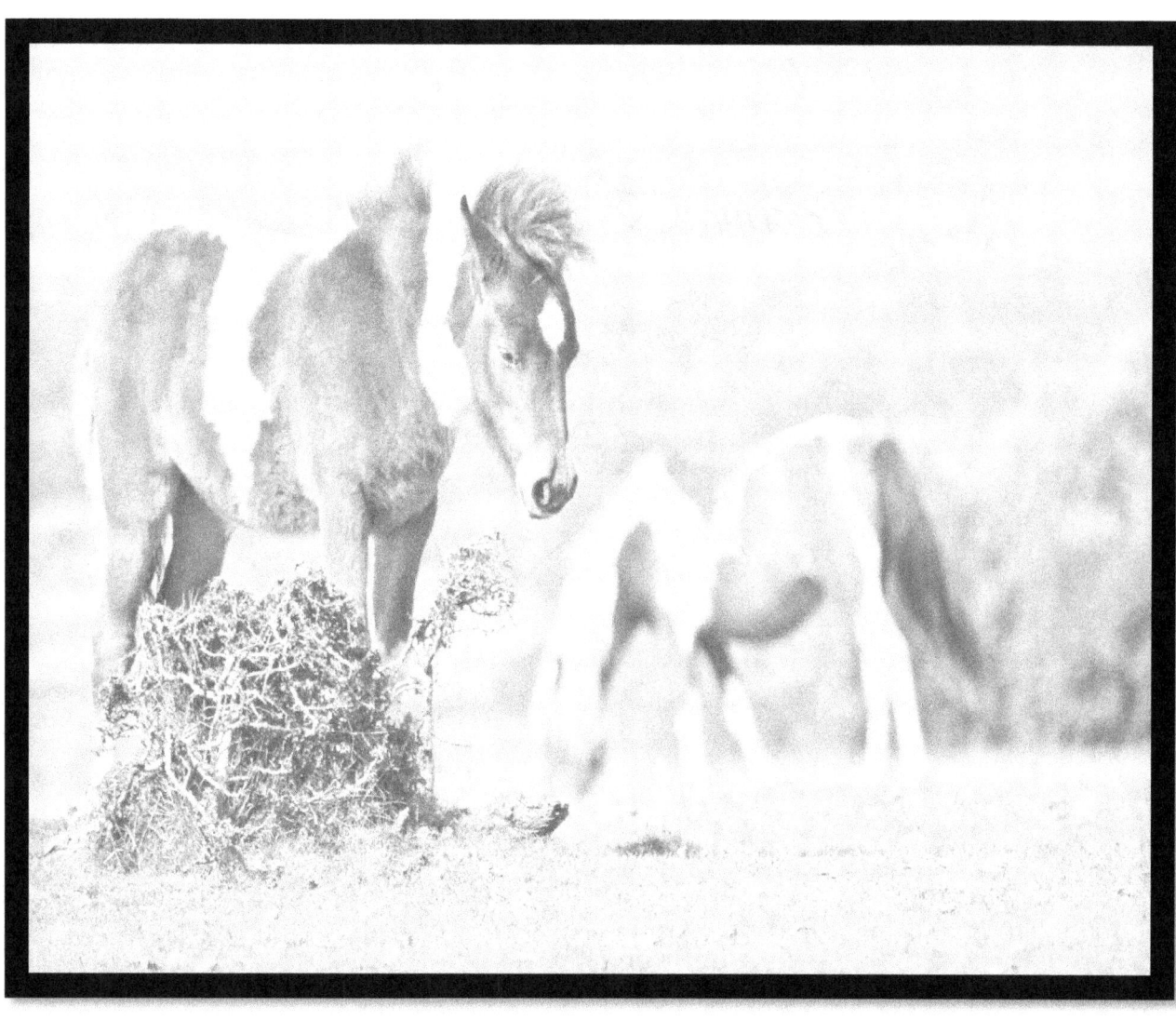

Coloring Book for Adults

Horses Lovers

By

Engy Khalil

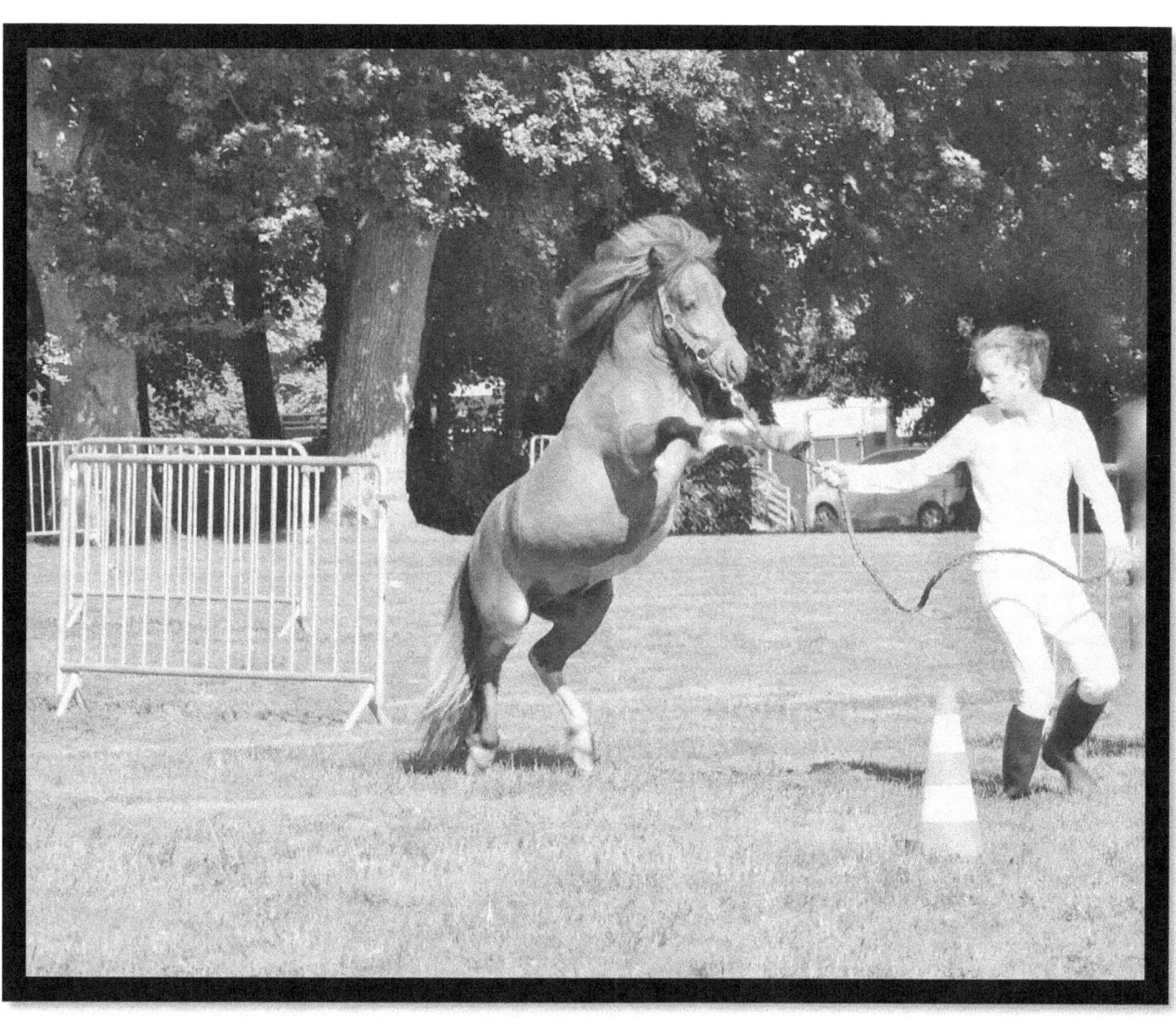

Coloring Book for Adults

Horses Lovers

By

Engy Khalil

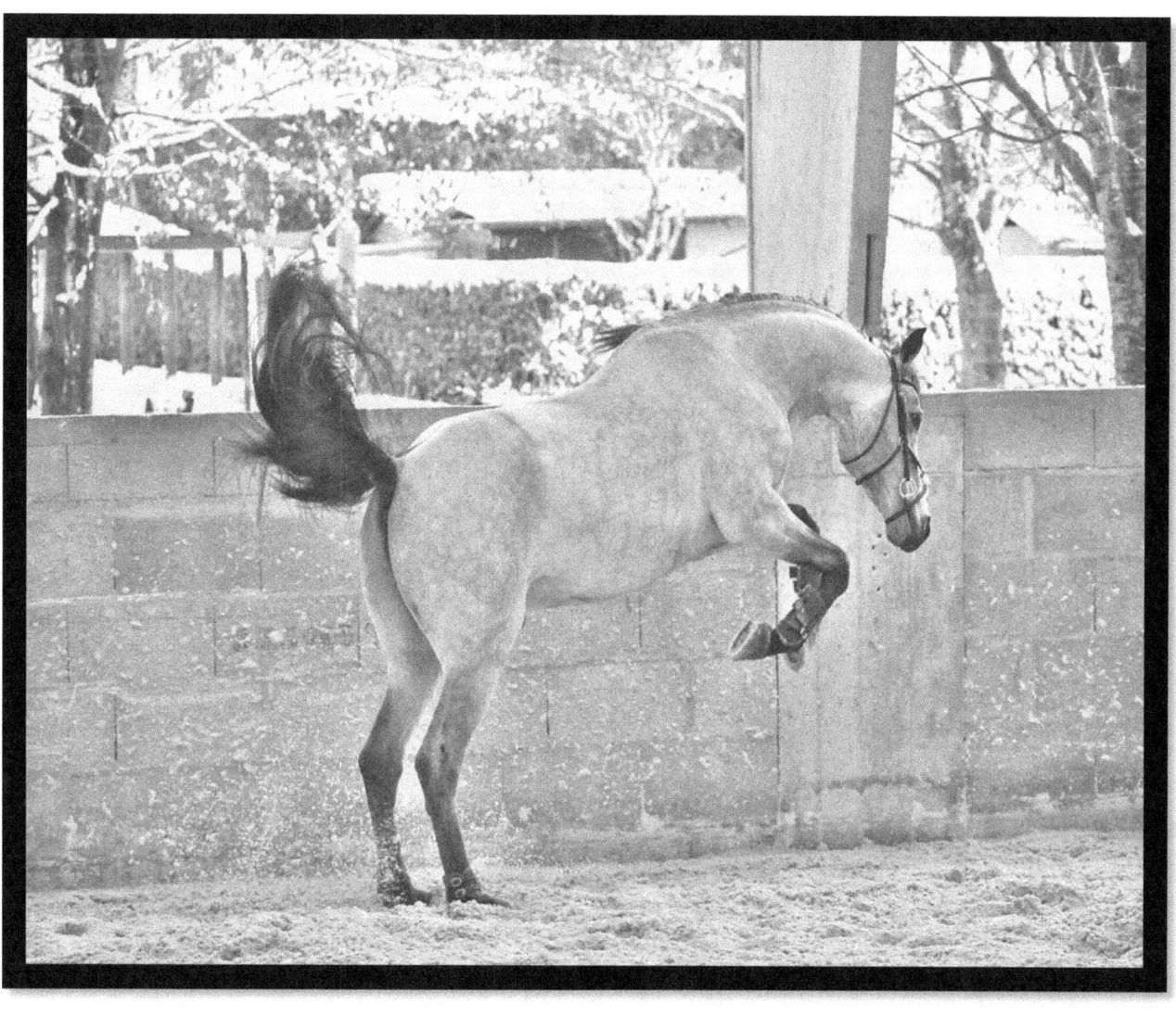

Coloring Book for Adults

Horses Lovers

By

Engy Khalil

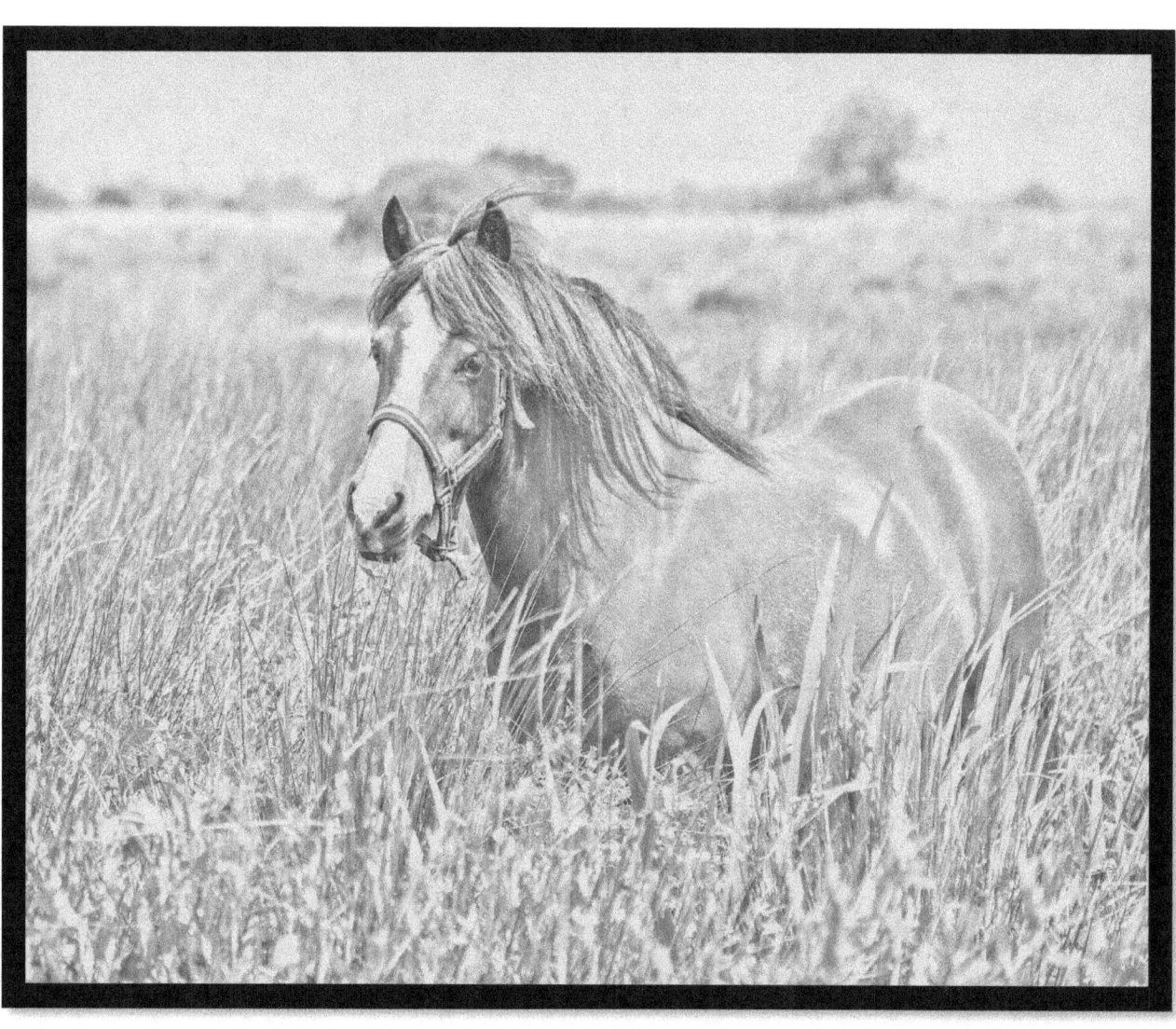

Coloring Book for Adults

Horses Lovers

By

Engy Khalil

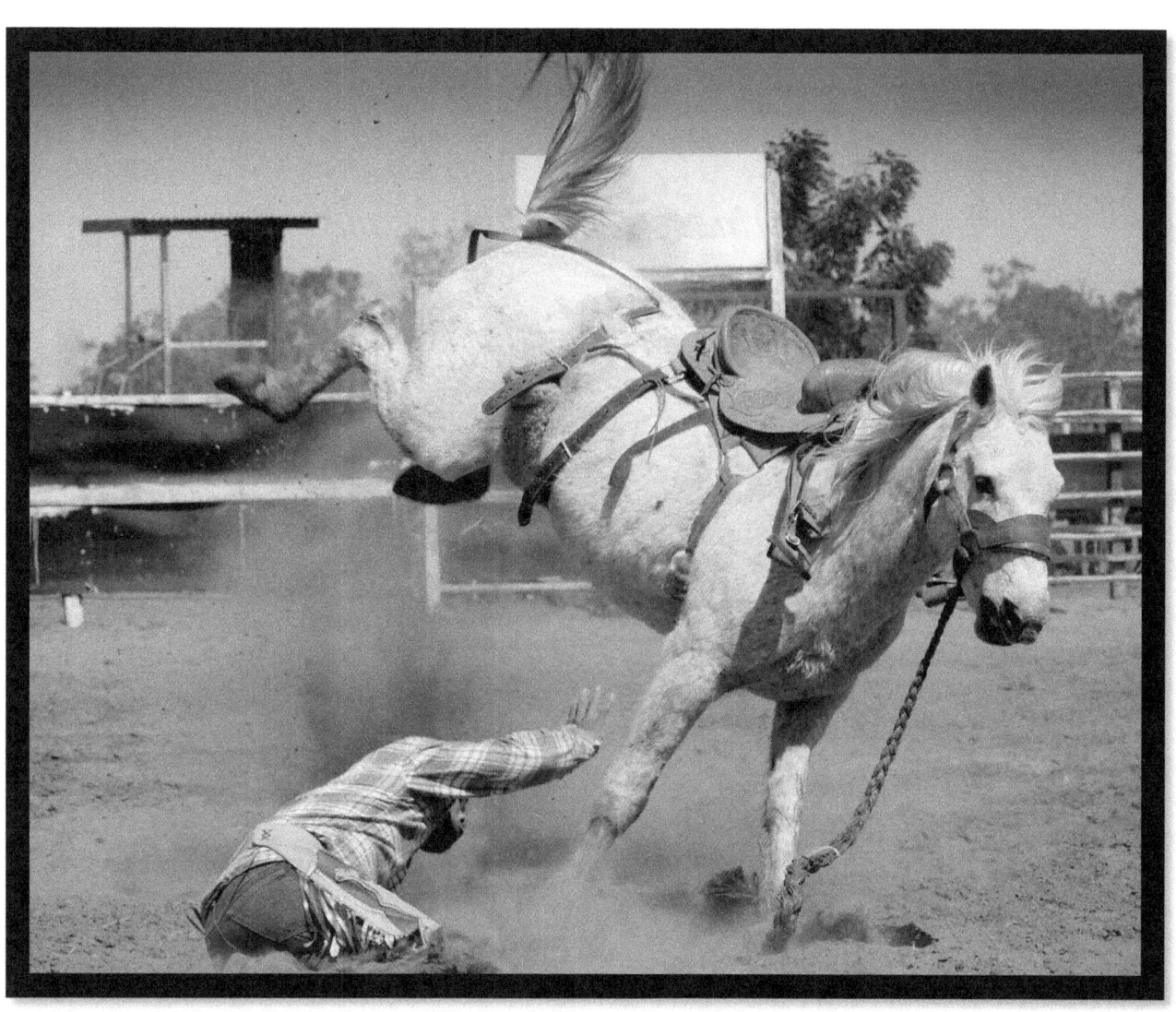

Coloring Book for Adults

Horses Lovers

By

Engy Khalil

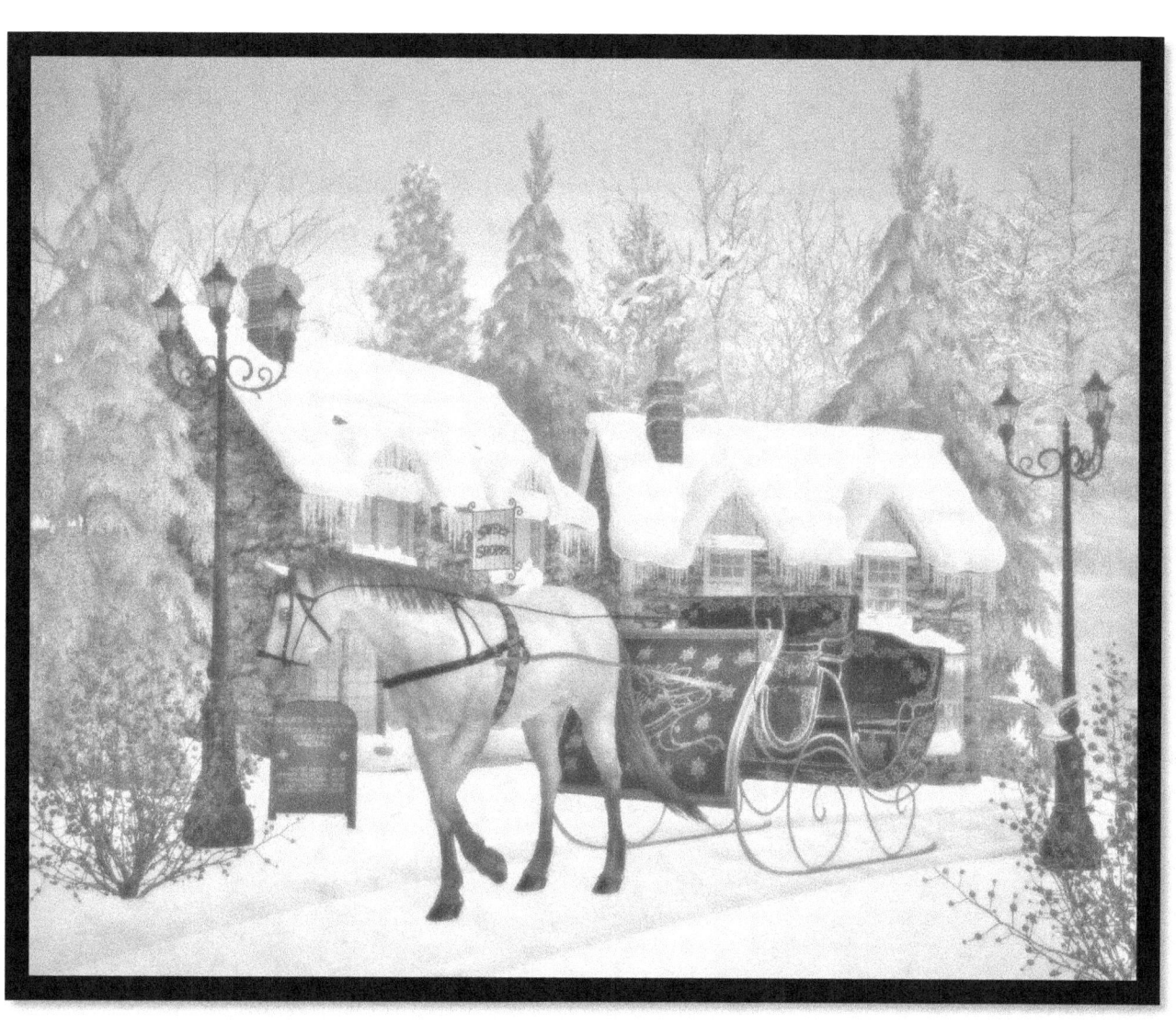

Coloring Book for Adults

Horses Lovers

By

Engy Khalil

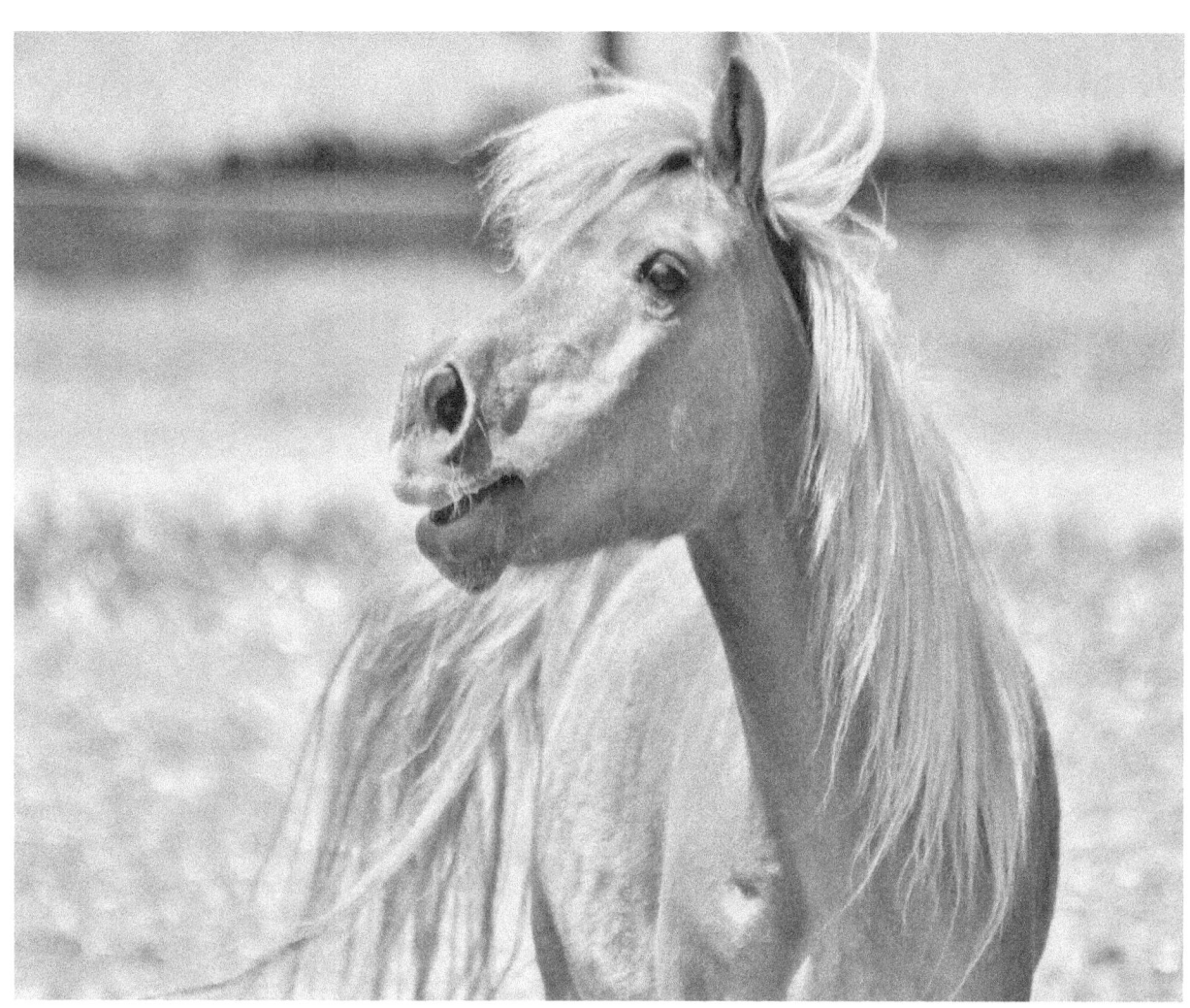

Coloring Book for Adults

Horses Lovers

By

Engy Khalil

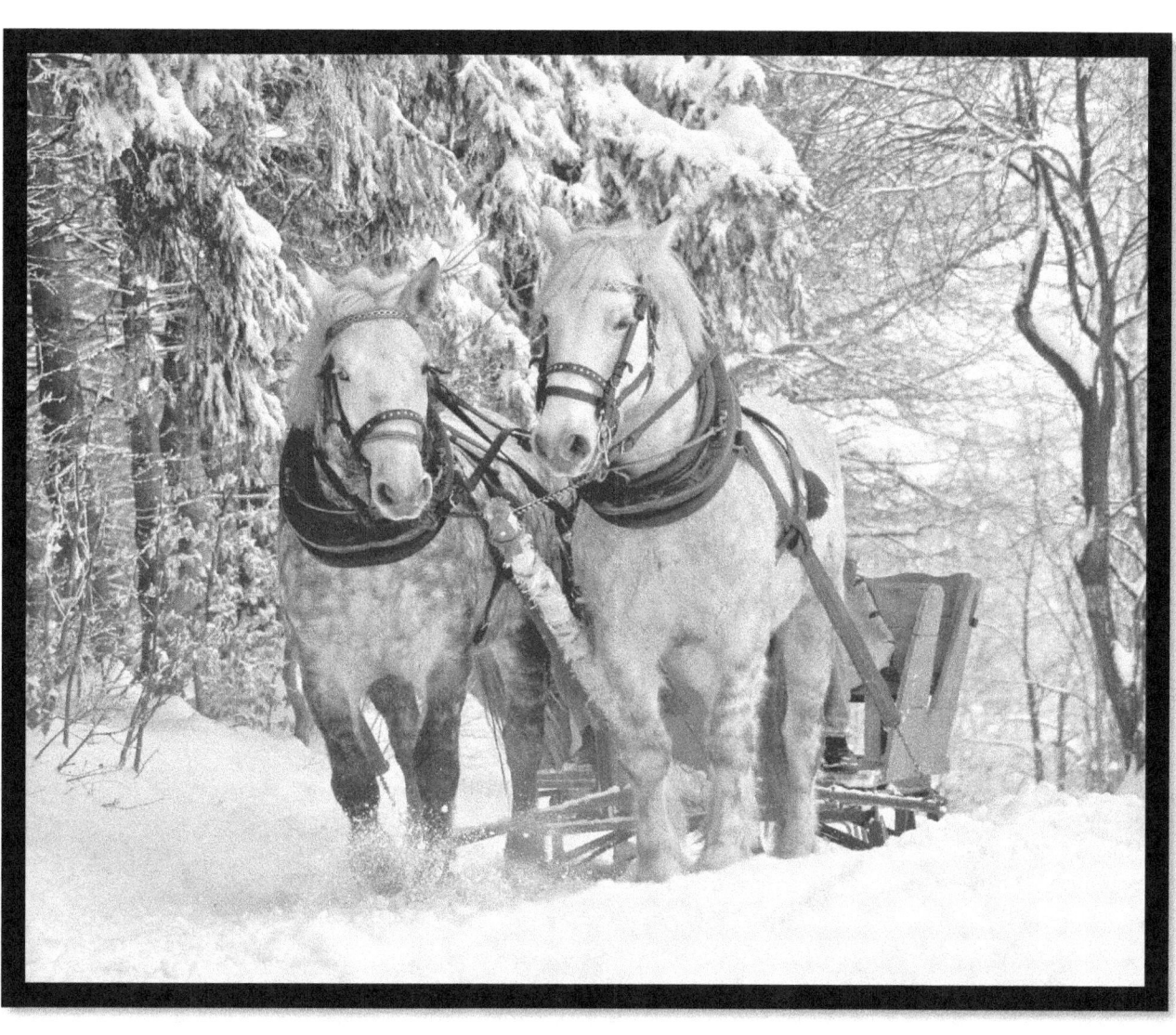

Coloring Book for Adults

Horses Lovers

By

Engy Khalil

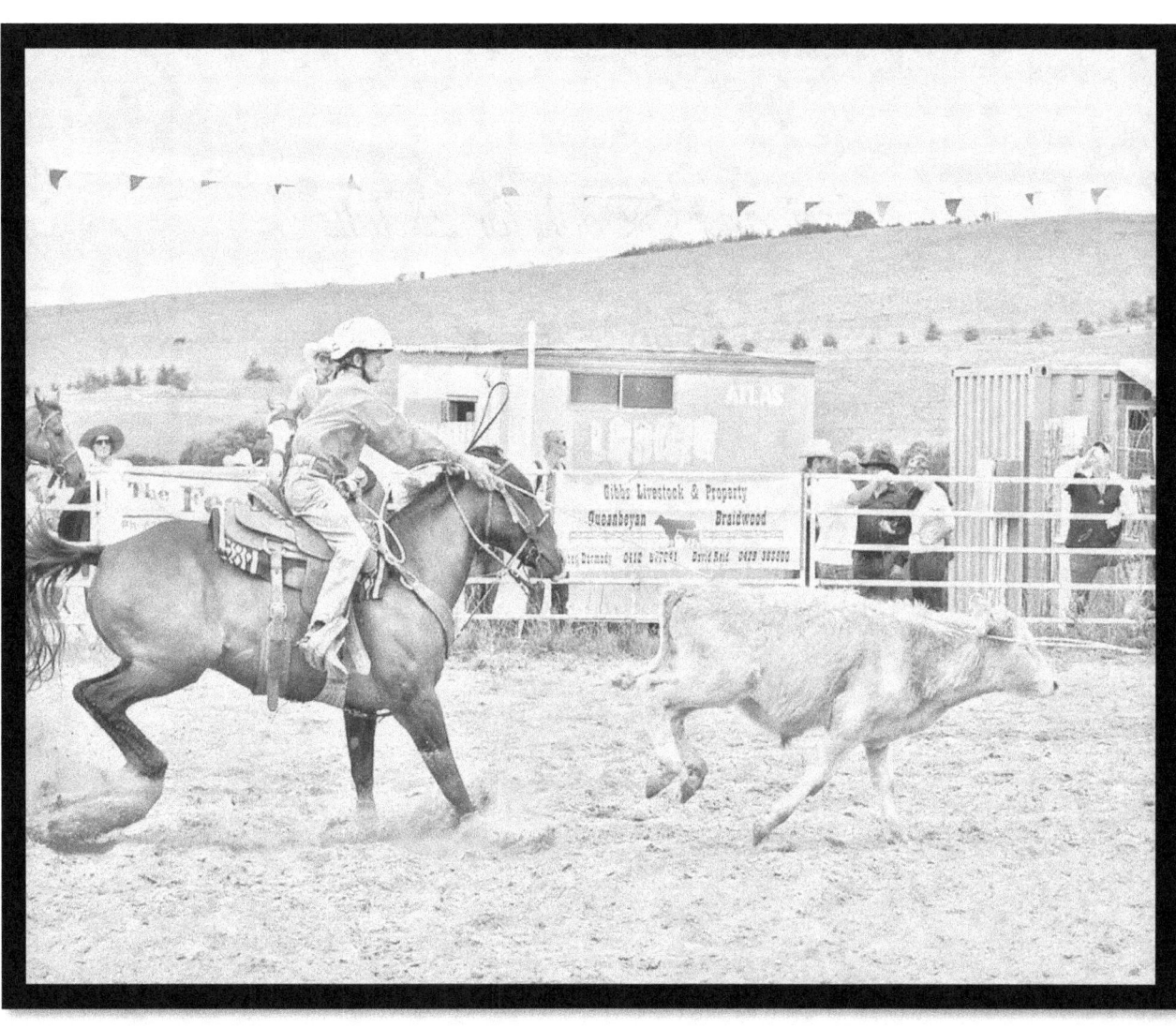

Coloring Book for Adults

Horses Lovers

By

Engy Khalil

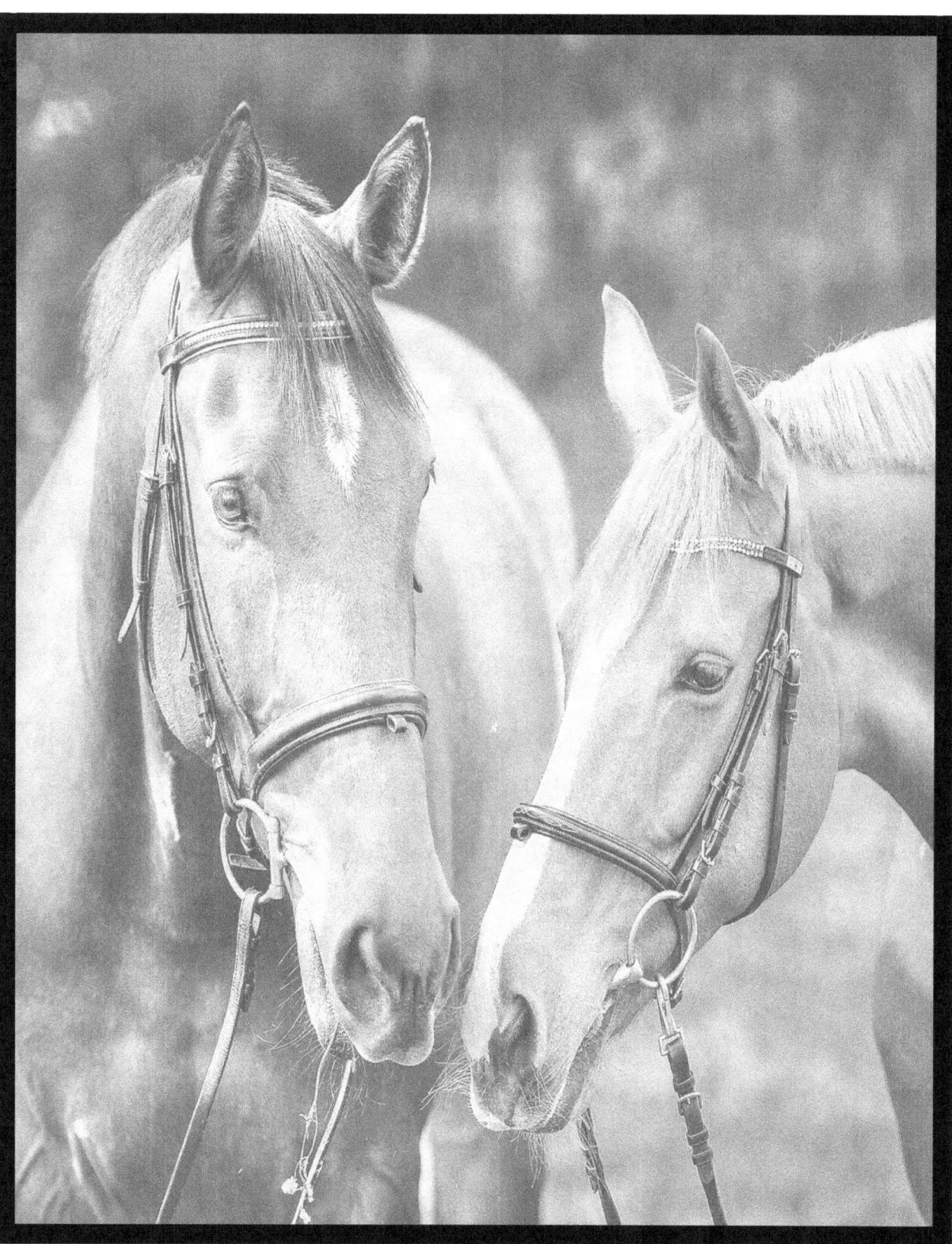

Coloring Book for Adults

Horses Lovers

By

Engy Khalil

Your Free Bonus from "the Coloring Book for Adults Dog Lovers" by Engy Khalil in the Next Pages!

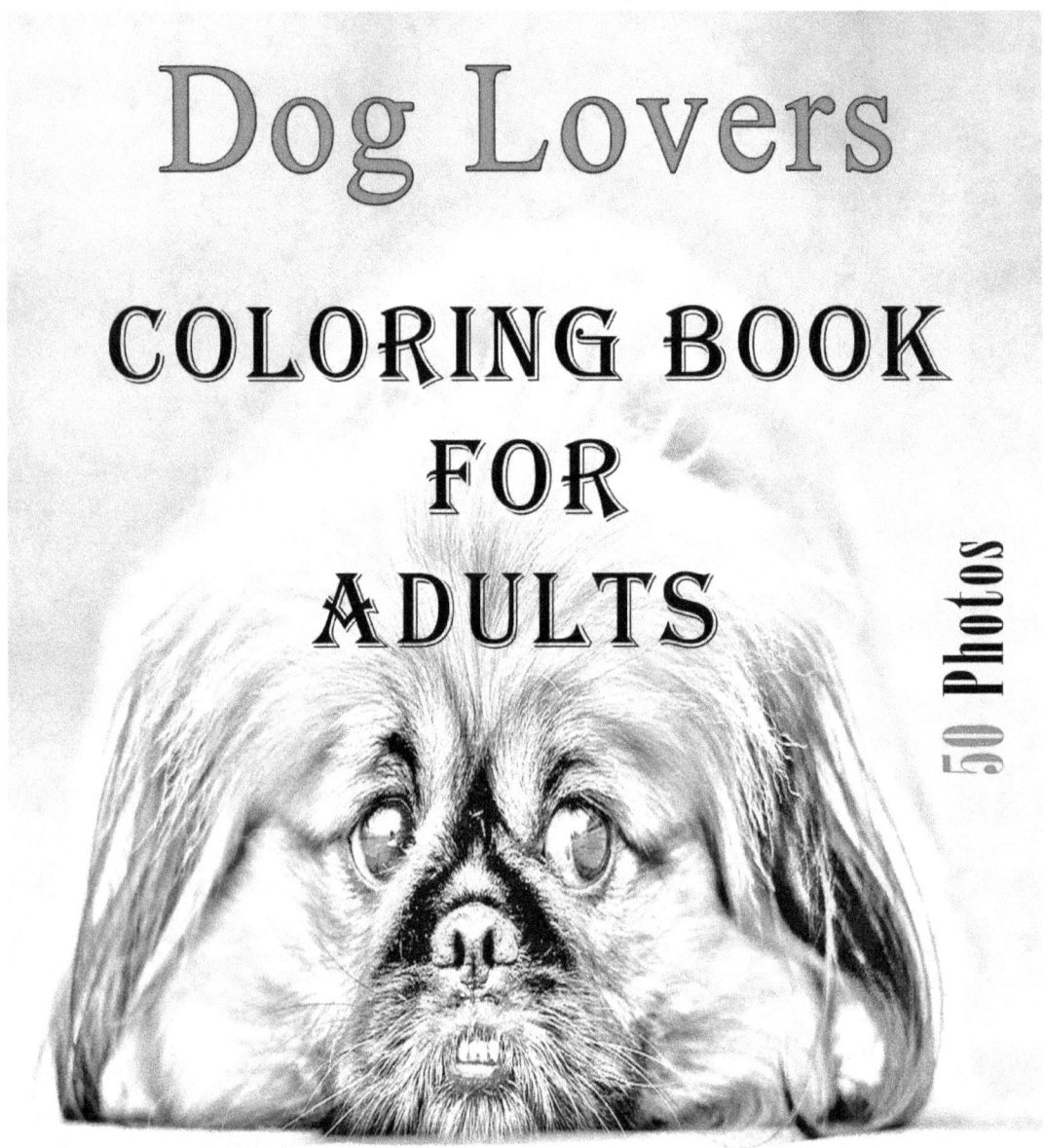

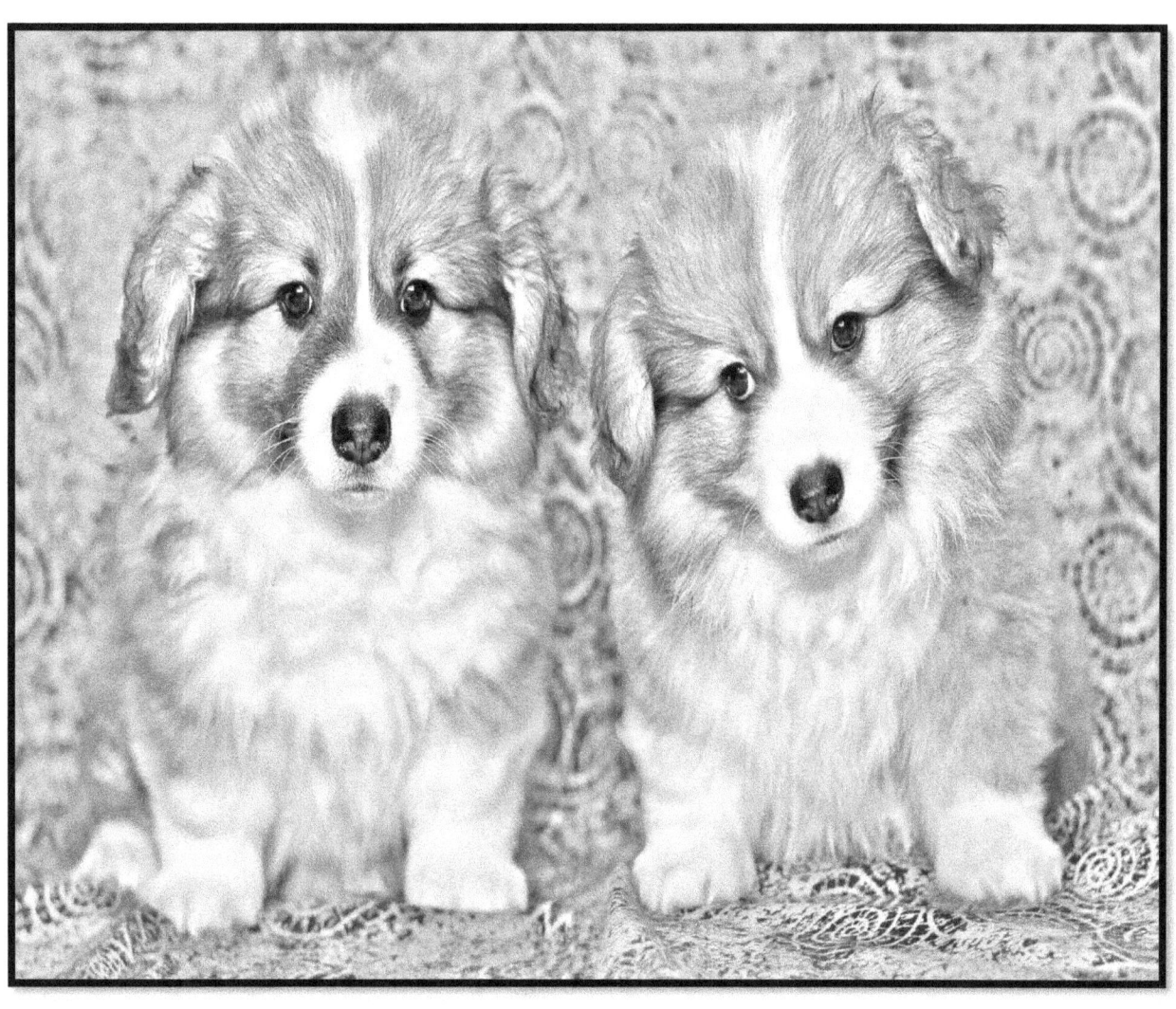

Coloring Book for Adults

Dog Lovers

By

Engy Khalil

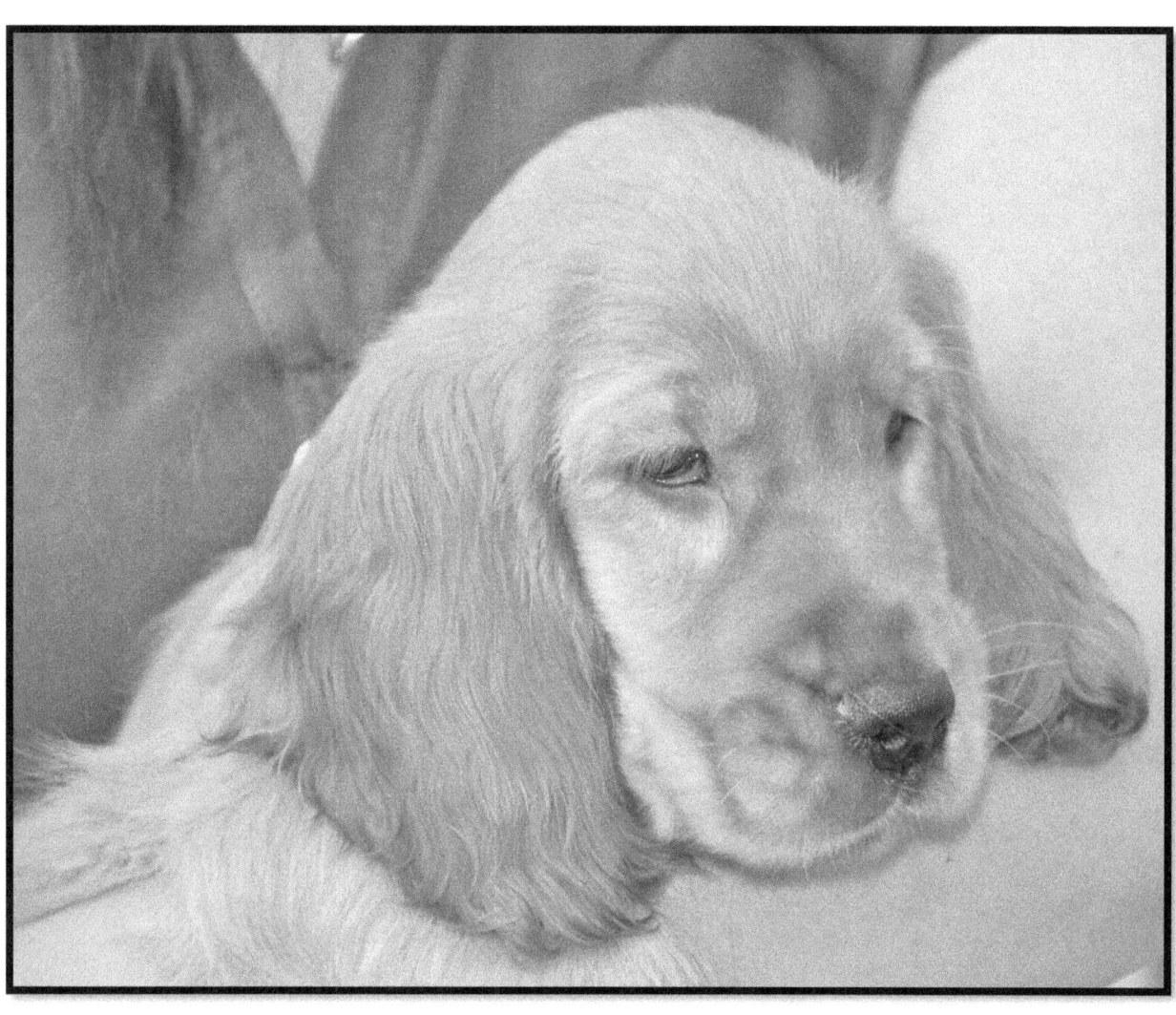

Coloring Book for Adults

Dog Lovers

By

Engy Khalil

Keep in Touch

For more coloring books, coloring ideas, tips and free coloring photos visit:

Adultscoloringbook.net

&

EBook-Book.com

Note:

If you liked this book please write your review.

Hope you enjoyed the book!

Engy Khalil

Test Your Colors Here!

Test Your Colors Here!

Test Your Colors Here!

www.ingramcontent.com/pod-product-compliance
Lightning Source LLC
Chambersburg PA
CBHW082339220526
45470CB00008B/2573